SIMPLE ASIAN COOKERY

KEN HOM

SIMPLE ASIAN COOKERY

KEN HOM

Step by step to everyone's
favourite recipes from Indonesia,
Malaysia, Singapore and Vietnam

BBC
BOOKS

About the author

Ken Hom is widely regarded as one of the world's greatest authorities on Oriental cooking. He has made several series for the BBC including *Chinese Cookery*, *Hot Wok*, *Travels with a Hot Wok* and *Foolproof Chinese Cookery*, and his many books are worldwide bestsellers. He is a consultant to Noble House Leisure Limited, which includes the Yellow River Cafés and signature restaurants. He lives in Paris, south-west France and Thailand.

Dedication

To my godson, Christian Eliott Mingde Oei, a true *bec fin*

Food photography by Jean Cazals

Published by BBC Books,
BBC Worldwide Ltd,
Woodlands, 80 Wood Lane,
London W12 0TT

First published in hardback as *Foolproof Asian Cookery* in 2003
This paperback edition first published in 2006
Reprinted 2006
Copyright © Promo Group Ltd 2003
The moral right of Ken Hom to be identified as the author of this work has been asserted.
Food photography © Jean Cazals 2003

ISBN-13: 978 0 563 49368 6
ISBN-10: 0 563 49368 2

Commissioning editor: Vivien Bowler
Project editor: Sarah Lavelle
Copy editor: Jane Middleton
Art direction and design: Lisa Pettibone
Production controller: Arlene Alexander
Home economist: Marie Ange Lapierre
Stylist: Sue Rowlands

The publishers would like to thank the following for supplying items used in the photographs: Kara Kara, David Mellor and William Levine

Set in Univers
Printed and bound in Italy by Printer Trento srl.
Colour separations by Kestrel Digital Colour, Chelmsford

Contents

Introduction

'Ethnic' cuisines – Indian, Chinese and Thai – have enjoyed increasing popularity throughout the West. Now more than ever, our cooking is being revitalized by an openness to outside influences, drawing upon foreign ingredients, flavours and techniques.

The growing Asian influences on Western cooking have aroused curiosity about other cuisines in the Far East too. Thus we are turning our attention to the lesser-known but equally delicious food of Indonesia, Malaysia, Singapore and Vietnam. Most of the ingredients for these cuisines are available in ordinary supermarkets and we can now profit from restaurants offering native dishes and menus. The result has been an expansion of culinary horizons for all of us.

What are the characteristics of these exotic cuisines? They are as varied as their individual cultures and history. Indonesia is an archipelago of more than 17,000 islands and is home to the world's fifth largest population. Its rich culinary history has been influenced at various times by the Chinese, Indians, Dutch, Portuguese and even the English. Many Indonesian dishes have a pungent, spicy taste balanced by sour, sweet and salty flavours, and tempered by fragrant lemon grass, chillies, fresh herbs and coconut milk.

The Malay peninsula enjoys a tropical climate and geography. No doubt this has had an impact on its cuisine as well. Malaysian cooking has heavy Chinese and Indian influences, which blend with Malay tradition to produce a very distinctive style. It is a fusion of stir-fried dishes with curries, tasty fried dishes and grilled marinated meats.

Singapore's unique position as a cosmopolitan crossroads is exemplified by its cuisine. Heavily influenced by Chinese food, mixed with Malay and Indian touches, Singaporean cooking is the ultimate fusion food. The tropical climate makes eating an outdoor affair. Stir-fried dishes, grilled meats, even steamed dishes are served all day and night on the streets and in the food courts that are such a feature of Singaporean dining. Vietnam borders China and Southeast Asian nations such as Laos and Cambodia. Its cuisine reflects the influences of its neighbours but is unusually delicate at the same time: soups are light yet complex, and full of herbaceous flavours; many dishes are complemented by dipping sauces that are salty, spicy and sour all at once.

Our knowledge of these four important cuisines not only enriches our culinary enjoyment but is a natural development of our interest in Chinese and Thai cooking, which we all love so much. I wish you a happy voyage on this exciting culinary adventure.

Ingredients and Equipment

INGREDIENTS

The cuisine of Southeast Asia – Vietnam, Malaysia, Indonesia and Singapore – has recently grown in popularity with home cooks and master chefs alike. Asian ingredients have become valued staples in the pantries of both home and restaurant kitchens. This is partly in response to health concerns, as most Asian cooking is light and clean, with little added animal fat such as cream, cheese or butter. Furthermore, with global connections now commonplace, many formerly exotic ingredients have become familiar and readily available. And, as Asian emigration has expanded throughout the West, Asian cooking has cross-pollinated with that of other cultures.

Below is a brief guide to Asian ingredients used in this book.

Beancurd

Also known as tofu, beancurd is highly nutritious and rich in protein, with a distinctive texture but bland taste. It is made from yellow soya beans, which are soaked, ground, mixed with water and then cooked briefly before being solidified. Beancurd is readily available in two forms – as firm cakes or as a thickish junket – and may also be found in several dried forms and in a fermented version. The soft, junket-like variety (sometimes called silken tofu) is used for stir-frying, braising and poaching. Solid beancurd 'cakes' are white in colour and are sold in supermarkets and Chinese grocer's shops, as well as in many healthfood shops. They are packed in water in plastic containers and may be kept in this state in the refrigerator for up to five days, provided the water is changed daily.

To use solid beancurd, cut it into cubes or shreds with a sharp knife. Do this with care, as it is delicate. It also needs to be cooked carefully, as too much stirring can cause it to crumble.

Chillies

Chillies are the seed pods of capsicum plants and can be obtained fresh, dried or ground. They come in many colours, hundreds of varieties, and varying degrees of intensity (heat) but the commercially available ones are few in number and one readily learns which are which and how to use them.

Some Asian cooks use chillies with reckless abandon but beginners should be more circumspect. It is perhaps best to begin 'cool' and gradually increase the heat. The seeds are the source of most of the heat. Removing them reduces the intensity but leaves a rich flavour.

Fresh chillies

Fresh chillies should look smooth and bright, with no brown patches or black spots. Red chillies are generally milder than green ones because they sweeten as they ripen. The small red or green Thai chillies are especially pungent, and can be fierily hot.

To prepare fresh chillies, rinse them under cold running water, then slit them lengthways with a small, sharp knife. Remove and discard the seeds. Rinse the chillies again, then prepare them according to the instructions in your recipe. Wash your hands, knife and chopping board before preparing other foods, and be careful not to touch your eyes until you have washed your hands thoroughly with soap and water.

Dried red chillies

Dried red chillies are small, thin and about 1 cm (1/2 in) long. They are normally left whole or cut in half lengthways with the seeds left in and used to season oil for stir-fried dishes, sauces and braises.

Dried chillies can be found in Thai and Chinese food shops, as well as in most supermarkets. They will keep indefinitely in a tightly covered jar.

Above: fresh and dried chillies

Above: Chinese leaves and preserved vegetables

Chilli powder

Chilli powder, also known as cayenne pepper, is made from dried red chillies and is extremely pungent. As with chillies in general, your own palate will determine the acceptable degree of heat for each dish when adding chilli powder. 'Use sparingly' are the watchwords for beginners.

Chinese dried mushrooms

There are many varieties of these, either black or brown, but the very large, pale ones with a cracked surface are the best. They are usually the most expensive, so use them sparingly. They are available in boxes or plastic bags from Chinese grocers. Store in an airtight jar. To use dried mushrooms, soak them in a bowl of warm water for about 20 minutes or until they are soft and pliable. Squeeze out the excess water, then cut off and discard the woody stems. Only the caps should be used. The soaking water can be saved and used in soups or for cooking rice. Strain it through a fine sieve to separate any sand or residue from the dried mushrooms.

Chinese leaves (Peking cabbage)

This delicious crunchy vegetable comes in various sizes, from long, compact, barrel-shaped ones to short, squat types. The heads are tightly packed with firm, pale green (or in some cases slightly yellow), crinkled leaves. It is most commonly added to soups and stir-fried meat dishes but its ability to absorb flavours and its pleasant taste and texture make it a favourite with chefs, who like to pair it with rich foods. Store it as you would ordinary cabbage.

Chinese preserved vegetables (preserved mustard greens)

Mustard greens are known in Chinese as 'greens heart' because only the heart of the plant is eaten – that is, the stem, buds and young leaves. They are quite unlike the mustard greens of the American South. These leaves are a vital part of the Chinese diet, being easy to cultivate and rich in vitamins and minerals. They are enjoyed year round, either fresh, or preserved with salt, water, vinegar and sugar. The preserved greens have a sweet and sour taste and are used as a vegetable or a flavouring ingredient, especially in soups. They can also be eaten as a snack or in stir-fries with meat, poultry or fish.

The best preserved vegetables can be found in large crocks in Chinese markets, which usually means they have been locally made. Alternatively, buy the ones in small crocks or cans, which come from Hong Kong, Taiwan or China. Once you have opened the crock or can, transfer the preserved vegetables to a glass jar and store in the refrigerator, where they will keep indefinitely.

Coconut milk

Coconut milk is used extensively throughout Southeast Asia. It has some of the properties of cow's milk – for example, the 'cream' (fatty globules) rises to the top when the milk sits; it must be stirred as it comes to the boil; and its fat is closer in chemical composition to butter fat than to vegetable fat. These qualities make it an important and unusual ingredient in Asian cookery.

The milk itself is the liquid wrung from pressed, grated coconut flesh, then combined with water. In Asian cooking it is used in curries and stews and is often combined with curry pastes to make sauces. It is also used as a popular cooling drink and a key ingredient in puddings and sweets.

In Southeast Asian markets and, more rarely, Chinese food shops, it may be possible to buy freshly made coconut milk, especially in neighbourhoods where there is a large Asian population. Inexpensive tinned coconut milk can be found in supermarkets and Asian food shops. Many brands are high quality and quite acceptable, particularly ones from Thailand or Malaysia. Be sure to shake the tin well before opening.

Coriander (Chinese parsley)

Fresh coriander is one of the most popular herbs used in Asian cooking. It looks like flat-leaf parsley but its pungent, musky, citrus-like flavour gives it a distinctive character that is unmistakable. It is an acquired taste for many people, but one worth the effort.

Its feathery leaves are often used as a garnish, or they can be chopped and mixed into sauces and stuffings. Fresh coriander is now widely available from supermarkets and greengrocers.

When buying fresh coriander, choose deep

green, fresh-looking leaves. Limp, yellowing leaves indicate age and should be avoided. To store coriander, wash it in cold water, drain it thoroughly (preferably in a salad spinner) and wrap it in kitchen paper. Keep it in the vegetable compartment of your refrigerator, where it should last for several days.

Coriander, ground

Ground coriander has a fresh, sweet, lemony taste and is widely used in curry mixes. It can be purchased already ground but, for the best flavour, toast whole coriander seeds in the oven and then grind them yourself.

Curry powder, Madras

Although Western-style curry powders and pastes are quite different from those used in Indian cuisine, there are many reliable commercial brands that serve very well. These are used by Asian cooks because their exotic flavours and subtle aromas add so much to any dish. Remember, curry is a term that refers to a style of cookery and not to a single taste or spice.

Five-spice powder

This is becoming a staple in the spice section of supermarkets, and Chinese grocers always keep it in stock. It is a mixture of ground star anise, Sichuan peppercorns, fennel, cloves and cinnamon. A good blend will be pungent, fragrant, spicy and slightly sweet. The exotic fragrance it gives to a dish makes the search for good five-spice powder well worth the effort. It keeps indefinitely in a tightly sealed jar.

Galangal

This rhizome is related to ginger and is commonly known as Thai or Siamese ginger. Creamy white in colour, with distinctive pink shoots, it has a hot, peppery flavour and is usually mixed with chillies and other spices and herbs to make a base for curries, soups and stews. If it is unavailable, substitute fresh ginger.

Garlic

This common, nutritious and very popular seasoning is used by Asian cooks in numerous ways – whole, finely chopped, crushed and pickled – to flavour curries, spicy sauces, soups, and practically every dish on the menu.

Select fresh garlic that is firm and preferably pinkish in colour. It should be stored in a cool, dry place but not the refrigerator, where it can easily become mildewed or begin sprouting.

Ginger

Fresh root ginger is an indispensable ingredient in Asian cookery. Its pungent, spicy taste adds a subtle but distinctive flavour to soups, meats and vegetables, and it is also an important seasoning for fish and seafood, since it neutralizes fishy aromas.

Root ginger looks rather like a gnarled Jerusalem artichoke and can vary in length from 7.5–15 cm (3–6 in) long. Select firm, unshrivelled pieces and peel off the skin before use. It will keep in the refrigerator, well wrapped in cling film, for up to 2 weeks. Fresh ginger can be bought at most Asian and Chinese markets, as well as at many greengrocers and supermarkets. Dried powdered ginger has a quite different flavour and is not an adequate substitute.

Kaffir lime leaves

From the kaffir lime tree, this ingredient is a Southeast Asian original. The lime itself is green and about the size of a small orange. Its juice is used in cooking but it is the leaves that are highly prized. They have a singular lemon-lime flavour, at the edge of bitter, and add a special dimension to many dishes, including curries, soups and stews. Used in sauces, they slowly release their citrus flavours during cooking. Substitute lime zest if kaffir lime leaves are unavailable.

Lemon grass

This herb is close to being the 'signature' ingredient of Far Eastern cookery. Its subtle, lemony fragrance and flavour impart a very special cachet to delicate foods. It is considered a medicinal agent as well as a spice, and is often prescribed for digestive disorders. Lemon grass is closely related to citronella grass. The latter, however, has a stronger oil content and is more likely to be used commercially in perfumes and as a mosquito repellent. The two should not be confused. Lemon grass is available both fresh and dried. Fresh lemon grass is sold in stalks up to 60 cm (2 feet) long – it looks like a very long spring onion. Most recipes use only the bottom few

Above: ginger (top) and galangal (bottom)

Above: lemon grass stalks and kaffir lime leaves

centimetres. It is a fibrous plant but this is no problem because what is wanted is its fragrance and taste, and the pieces are always removed after the dish is cooked. Some recipes may call for lemon grass to be finely chopped or pounded into a paste, in which cases it becomes an integral part of the dish.

Try to buy the freshest possible lemon grass, which is usually found in Thai or other Asian food shops; it is becoming increasingly available in many supermarkets, too. Avoid dried lemon grass for cooking, as it is used mostly for herbal teas. Fresh lemon grass can be kept, loosely wrapped, in the bottom of the refrigerator for up to one week. Please note that lemon cannot be used as a substitute for the unique flavour of lemon grass.

Noodles

Noodles, like rice, form the basis of nutritious, quick, sustaining meals. Several styles of noodle dishes have now made their way to the West, including ones made with thin fresh egg noodles, or thicker egg or wheat noodles, as well as the popular rice noodles. Both fresh and dried kinds are available in Chinese shops and supermarkets.

Bean-thread (transparent) noodles

Also called cellophane noodles, these very fine white noodles are made from ground mung beans. They are available dried, packed in neat, plastic-wrapped bundles, from Chinese food shops and supermarkets.

Bean-thread noodles are never served on their own but are added to soups or braises or deep-fried and used as a garnish. Soak them in warm water for about 5 minutes before use. As they are rather long, you might find it easier to cut them into shorter lengths after soaking. If you are frying them, they do not need soaking beforehand but they do need to be separated. The best way to do this is to pull them apart in a large paper bag, which prevents them flying all over the place.

Rice noodles

These dried noodles are opaque white and come in a variety of shapes and thicknesses. One of the most common is rice stick noodles, which are flat and about the length of a chopstick. Rice noodles are very easy to prepare. Simply soak them in warm water for 20

minutes, until they are soft, then drain in a colander or a sieve. They are now ready to be used in soups or stir-fries.

Wheat noodles and egg noodles

Available dried or fresh, these are made from hard or soft wheat flour, water and sometimes egg, in which case they are labelled egg noodles. Flat noodles are usually used in soups, while round ones are best for frying. The fresh ones freeze well if they are tightly wrapped. Thaw thoroughly before cooking.

Dried wheat or fresh egg noodles are very good blanched and served as an accompaniment to main dishes instead of plain rice. If you are cooking noodles ahead of time or before stir-frying them, toss the drained cooked noodles in 2 teaspoons of sesame oil and put them in a bowl. Cover with cling film and refrigerate for up to 2 hours.

Clockwise from bottom: bean-thread, rice, rice-stick and egg noodles

Oils

Oil is the most commonly used cooking medium in Southeast Asia. My favourite is groundnut oil, but many Asian cooks use simple vegetable oil made from rapeseed.

Groundnut oil

This is also known as peanut oil or arachide oil. I prefer to use it for all types of cooking because it has a pleasant, unobtrusive taste. Although it has a higher saturated fat content than some oils, its ability to be heated to a high temperature without burning makes it perfect for stir-frying and deep-frying. Most supermarkets stock groundnut oil, but if you cannot find it, use corn oil instead.

Corn oil

Corn or maize oil is also quite suitable for this type of cooking, since it has a high heating point. However, I find it rather bland and with a slightly disagreeable smell. It is high in polyunsaturates and is therefore one of the healthier oils.

Above: raw prawns

Other vegetable oils

Some of the cheaper vegetable oils available include soya bean, safflower and sunflower. They are light in colour and taste, and can also be used in Asian cooking, but take care, since they smoke and burn at lower temperatures than groundnut oil.

Sesame oil

This thick, rich, golden brown oil made from sesame seeds has a distinctive, nutty flavour and aroma. It is widely used as a seasoning but is not normally used as a cooking oil because it burns easily. Therefore, think of it more as a flavouring than a cooking oil. A small amount is often added at the last moment to finish a dish.

Peppercorns

Black peppercorns

Black peppercorns are unripe berries from a vine, *Piper nigrum*, which are picked, fermented and then dried until they are hard and black. They are best when freshly ground. Until chillies were introduced into Southeast Asia in the sixteenth century, black pepper provided the 'heat' in Asian cooking.

White peppercorns

White peppercorns are made from the largest ripe berries, which are suspended in running water for several days until they swell up so that the skin can be removed more easily. The pale seeds are sun-dried, which turns them a pale beige colour – hence 'white' peppercorns.

Prawns

For the recipes in this book you will need large raw prawns, usually sold as Pacific or king prawns. Most Chinese food shops, many fishmongers and some supermarkets stock them frozen in the shell, and they are quite reasonably priced. Fresh prawns are also available but these tend to have been cooked and, in many cases, overcooked. Frozen raw prawns are preferable, as the ready-cooked ones will not absorb the flavours of the sauce you cook them in.

To shell prawns, twist off and discard the head, then open up the shell along the belly and peel if off, together with the tiny legs (the tail shell can be left on for an attractive presentation, if liked). Large prawns should also be de-veined by making a shallow cut down the back of each prawn and pulling out the fine digestive vein that runs along it. Wash the prawns before use.

A Chinese trick for improving frozen raw prawns after shelling and de-veining is to rinse them three times in 1 tablespoon of salt and 1.2 litres (2 pints) cold water, changing the salt and water each time. This helps to firm the texture of the prawns and gives them a crystalline, clean taste.

Rice

There are many different types of rice in the Far East but long-grain is the most popular. Look for basmati or any other superior long-grain white rice, which will be dry and fluffy when cooked. Avoid pre-cooked or 'easy-cook' rice, as it lacks the full flavour and the texture of good long-grain rice.

The secret of preparing rice without it becoming sticky is to cook it first in an uncovered pot at a high heat until most of the water has evaporated. Then the heat should be turned very low, the pan covered, and the rice cooked slowly in the remaining steam. Never uncover the pan once the steaming process has begun; just time it and wait.

Here is a good trick to remember: if you cover the rice with about 2.5 cm (1 in) of water, it should always cook properly without sticking. Many packet recipes for rice use too much water, resulting in a gluey mess. Follow my method and you will have perfect steamed rice.

For 4 people you will need enough long-grain rice to fill a measuring jug to 400 ml (14 fl oz). Put the rice in a large bowl and wash it in several changes of water until the water becomes clear. Drain the rice, put it into a heavy pan with 600 ml (1 pint) water and bring to the boil. Boil for about 5 minutes, until most of the surface liquid has evaporated. The surface of the rice should have small indentations, like a pitted crater. At this point, cover the pan with a very tight-fitting lid, turn the heat as low as possible and let the rice cook undisturbed for 15 minutes. There is no need to 'fluff' the rice; just let it rest off the heat for 5 minutes before serving.

Rice paper

Rice paper is made from a mixture of rice flour, water and salt, which is rolled out by

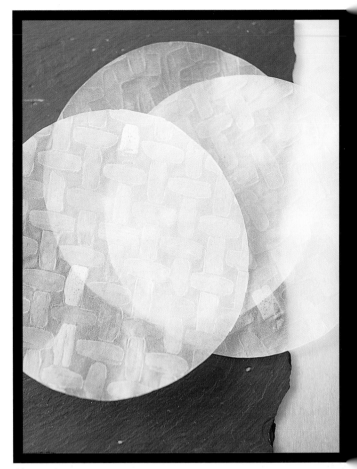

Above: rice paper

machine until paper-thin, then dried on bamboo mats in the sun, giving the translucent sheets their beautiful cross-hatch imprint. It is used extensively for wrapping spring rolls, particularly in Vietnam. I prefer to use rice paper rather than wheat-based wrappers, as it absorbs less oil when deep-fried.

Rice paper is available from Chinese and Thai food shops, in packets of 50–100 round or triangular sheets. All brands are good, especially the ones from Vietnam and Thailand. Choose white-looking rice paper and avoid yellowish ones, which may be too old. Broken pieces in the packet may also indicate age.

Store rice paper in a cool, dry place. After use, wrap the remaining rice papers carefully in the pack they came in, put this in a plastic bag and seal well before storing.

Salted black beans

These small black soya beans are fermented with salt and spices to preserve them. Their distinctive flavour makes them a tasty seasoning, especially when used with garlic or fresh ginger. They are inexpensive and can be obtained from Chinese grocers, usually in tins labelled 'black beans in salted sauce', but you may also see them packed in plastic bags. You can rinse them before use as an optional step; I prefer to chop them slightly, too, as this helps to release their pungent flavour. Transfer any unused beans and liquid to a sealed jar and they will keep indefinitely in the refrigerator. For convenience, black bean sauce is now available in supermarkets, which in many cases is authentic and quite acceptable.

Sauces and pastes

Asian cookery involves a number of tasty sauces and pastes, some light, some thick. They are essential for authentic Asian cooking, and it is well worth making the effort to obtain them. Most are sold in bottles or tins in Chinese food shops and some supermarkets.

Above: chilli bean sauce

Once opened, tinned sauces should be transferred to screw-top glass jars and kept in the refrigerator, where they will last indefinitely.

Chilli bean sauce

This thick, dark sauce or paste is made from soya beans, chillies and other seasonings, and is very hot and spicy. Be sure to seal the jar tightly after use and store it in the larder or refrigerator. Do not confuse it with chilli sauce (see below), which is a hotter, redder, thinner sauce.

Chilli sauce

This hot, bright-red sauce, made from chillies, vinegar, sugar and salt, is mainly used as a dipping sauce. There are various brands available and you should experiment until you find the one you like best. If you find chilli sauce too strong, dilute it with hot water. Do not confuse this sauce with chilli bean sauce (see above), which is a much thicker, darker sauce used for cooking.

Fish sauce

Fish sauce is also known as fish gravy. It is a thin, brown sauce made from fermented salted fish, usually anchovies, and has a noticeably fishy odour and salty taste. If you are not used to it, add it sparingly at first. Bear in mind, though, that cooking greatly diminishes its fishy flavour, and the sauce does add a special richness and quality to dishes. The Thai brands, labelled *nam pla*, are especially good, with a less salty taste. Fish sauce is an inexpensive ingredient, so buy the best on offer.

Shrimp paste/shrimp sauce

This sauce is made from pulverized salted shrimp that is left to ferment. For shrimp paste, the mixture is dried in the sun and cut into cakes. Shrimp sauce, however, is packed directly into jars while thick and moist. Once packed, the light pink sauce slowly turns a greyish shade, acquiring a pungent flavour as it matures. Popular in Southeast Asian cooking, it adds a distinctive flavour and fragrance to dishes – similar to anchovy paste but stronger.

Although the odour of shrimp sauce is assertive, remember that the cooking process quickly tames its aroma and taste. The Chinese version is very good. Stored in the refrigerator, it will last indefinitely.

Clockwise from top: chilli sauce, dark soy sauce, light soy sauce and shrimp paste

Soy sauce

Soy sauce is an essential ingredient in Asian cooking. It is made from a mixture of soya beans, flour and water, which is fermented naturally and aged for some months. The liquid that is finally distilled is soy sauce.

There are two main types. Light soy sauce, as the name implies, is light in colour, but it is full of flavour and is the better one to use for cooking. It is saltier than dark soy sauce, and is known in Chinese food shops as Superior Soy.

Dark soy sauce, confusingly, is known as Soy Superior Sauce – I like that; both versions are 'superior'. The dark version is aged for much longer than light soy sauce, hence its darker, almost black colour, and it is also slightly thicker and stronger. It is more suitable for stews. I prefer it to light soy as a dipping sauce.

Most soy sauces sold in supermarkets are dark soy. Chinese food shops sell both types and the quality is excellent. Be sure you buy the correct one, as the names are very similar.

Shallots

These mild-flavoured members of the onion family are very popular in Southeast Asia, where the local versions are readily available. They are small – about the size of pickling onions – with copper-red skins, and have a distinctive onion flavour without being as strong or overpowering as ordinary onions. Western-style shallots make an excellent substitute for authentic Asian shallots, which can be difficult to find. They are quite expensive, but their sweet flavour permeates food, and a few go a long way. Keep them in a cool, dry place (not the refrigerator) and peel, slice or chop them as you would an onion.

Shaoxing rice wine

As a seasoning, wine is not essential to the cooking of the Far East, apart from Singapore, which has a strong Chinese culinary heritage. Rice wine has been a crucial ingredient in Chinese cooking for centuries, and I believe the finest of its many varieties is produced in Shaoxing in Zhejiang Province in eastern China. It is made from glutinous rice, yeast and spring water. Now readily available in Chinese markets and in some wine shops in the West, it should be kept tightly corked at room temperature. A good-quality, pale dry sherry can be substituted but cannot match rice wine's rich, mellow taste.

Do not confuse this wine with sake, which is the Japanese version of rice wine and quite different. Western grape wines are not an adequate substitute for either.

Spring onions

Spring onions can be prepared in a variety of ways, both for cooking and for garnish. First, peel off the outer layer if it is bruised or damaged, then trim the top and bottom.

To chop finely, split into quarters lengthways, then chop into small pieces horizontally. To shred, cut the onions in half horizontally, then split very finely lengthways. To curl shredded spring onions, put them in a bowl of ice-cold water. This makes an attractive garnish. Spring onions can also be cut simply on the round at various thicknesses, and also on the diagonal, which is useful for certain recipes and looks pretty as a garnish.

Star anise

Star anise is a hard, star-shaped spice, the seed pod of an attractive bush. It is similar in flavour and fragrance to common anise but more robust and liquorice-like. Star anise is an essential ingredient in five-spice powder (see page 12) and is widely used in braised dishes, to which it imparts a rich taste and fragrance. It is available in plastic packs from Chinese grocers and should be stored in a sealed jar in a cool, dry place.

Sugar

Sugar has been used – sparingly – in the cooking of savoury dishes in Southeast Asia for centuries. Properly employed, it helps balance the flavours of sauces and other dishes. Palm sugar, which comes as brown sugar slabs or in large lumps, is rich, with a more subtle flavour than refined granulated sugar, and gives a good lustre to braised dishes and sauces. It is available in packets from Chinese grocers, although some chefs prefer the quality of the canned version. You may need to break it into smaller pieces with a wooden mallet or rolling pin. If you cannot find palm sugar, use white sugar or coffee sugar crystals (the amber, chunky kind) instead. Light brown sugar mixed with an equal quantity of molasses may also serve as a substitute.

Vinegar

Vinegars are widely used in Southeast Asian cooking. Unlike Western vinegars, they are usually made from rice. There are many varieties, ranging in flavour from spicy and slightly tart to sweet and pungent. They can be bought in Chinese food shops and will keep indefinitely.

In some Asian recipes, chefs have taken to using a good-quality Western-style white vinegar, prized for its sharp tang. But never simply substitute white vinegar for rice vinegar; the contrast is too great. If you cannot get these vinegars, I suggest you use cider vinegar. Malt vinegar can be used, but its taste is stronger and more acidic.

White rice vinegar

This clear vinegar has a mild flavour with a faint taste of glutinous rice. It is used for sweet and sour dishes.

Black rice vinegar

Black rice vinegar is very dark in colour and rich, though mild, in taste. It is used for braised dishes, sauces, and sometimes as a dipping sauce for crab.

Red rice vinegar

This is sweet and spicy, and is normally used as a dipping sauce for seafood.

Above: spring onions (from top) finely chopped, shredded, cut on the round, cut on the diagonal

EQUIPMENT

Special equipment is not essential for cooking the food of Southeast Asia. Despite the complexities of ingredients, colours, tastes and textures, preparing Asian food is very straightforward.

However, there are a few tools, tested over many centuries of use, that will make the task very much easier. Once you become familiar with woks, for example, you will have already entered the culinary world of Southeast Asia. As a bonus, you will find that such tools are just as helpful in preparing your own favourite dishes.

Wok

Like the Chinese, the people of Vietnam, Malaysia, Indonesia and Singapore use the wok in preparing almost every meal. The most versatile piece of cooking equipment ever invented, it may be used for stir-frying, blanching, deep-frying and steaming. Its shape permits fuel-efficient, quick and even cooking. When stir-frying, the deep sides prevent the food spilling over; when deep-frying, much less oil is required because of the wok's tapered base.

There are two basic types: the traditional Cantonese version, with short, rounded handles on either side, and the *pau*, sometimes called the Peking wok, which has one 30–35 cm (12–14 in) long handle. The long-handled wok keeps you at a safer distance from splashing hot oil or water.

The standard round-bottomed wok may be used only on gas hobs. Ones with flatter bottoms are now available, designed especially for electric hobs. Although this shape really defeats the purpose of the traditional design, which is to concentrate intense heat at the centre, it does have the advantage over ordinary frying-pans because it has deeper sides.

Choosing a wok

Choose a large wok, preferably about 30–35 cm (12–14 in) in diameter, with deep sides. It is easier – and safer – to cook a small batch of food in a large wok than a large quantity in a small one.

Be aware that some modernized woks are too shallow or too flat-bottomed and thus little better than a frying-pan. A heavier wok, preferably made of carbon steel, is superior to the lighter stainless steel or aluminium type, which cannot take very high heat and tends to blacken, as well as scorch the food. Good non-stick carbon steel woks that maintain the heat without sticking are now available. They need special care to prevent scratching but in recent years non-stick technology has improved vastly so that they can now be safely recommended. They are especially useful when cooking food that has a high acid content, such as lemons.

Thai woks are generally made of brass and have a wider, flatter base. But they essentially do the same job as the Chinese wok.

Above, top to bottom: wok lid, cooking chopsticks, spatula, wok with rack, wooden spatula and cleaver

Seasoning a wok

All woks except non-stick ones should be seasoned before first use. Many need to be scrubbed as well, to remove the machine oil that is applied to the surface by the manufacturer to protect it in transit. This is the only time you will ever need to scrub your wok – unless you let it become rusty.

Scrub it with a cream cleanser and water to remove as much of the machine oil as possible. Then dry it and put it on the hob on a low heat. Add 2 tablespoons of cooking oil and, using a wad of kitchen paper, rub the oil over the inside of the wok until the entire surface is lightly coated. Heat the wok slowly for about 10–15 minutes and then wipe it thoroughly with more kitchen paper. The paper will become blackened from the machine oil. Repeat this process of coating, heating and wiping until the kitchen paper comes away clean. Your wok will darken and become well seasoned with use, which is a good sign.

Cleaning a wok

Once your wok has been seasoned, you should never scrub it with soap or water. Just wash it in plain clean water and dry it thoroughly after each use – putting the cleaned wok over a low heat for a minute or two should do the trick. If it does rust a bit, scrub it with a cream cleanser and re-season it. With ordinary usage and care, the versatile wok will serve you faithfully through countless meals.

Stir-frying in a wok

The most important thing when stir-frying is to have all your ingredients ready and to hand – this is a very fast method of cooking and you will not have time to stop and chop things. Heat the wok until it is very hot, then add the oil and distribute it evenly over the surface using a metal spatula or long-handled spoon. It should be very hot – almost smoking – before you add the ingredients.

Add the food to be cooked and stir-fry by tossing it around the wok with a metal spatula or long-handled spoon. If you are stir-frying meat, let each side rest for a few seconds before continuing to stir. Keep moving the food from the centre of the wok to the sides. I prefer to use a long-handled wok, as there can be a lot of splattering due to the high temperature at which the food must be cooked.

Wok accessories

Wok stand

This is a metal ring or frame designed to keep a conventionally shaped wok steady on the hob. It is essential if you want to use your wok for steaming, deep-frying or braising. Stands come in two designs: a solid metal ring punched with about six ventilation holes, and a thin, circular wire frame. If you have a gas cooker, use only the latter type, as the more solid design does not allow for sufficient ventilation and may lead to a build-up of gas, which could put the flame out completely.

Wok lid

This light, inexpensive domed cover, usually made from aluminium, is used for steaming. It is normally supplied with the wok, but if not, it may be purchased at a Chinese or Asian supermarket, or you may use any domed saucepan lid that fits snugly.

Spatula

A long-handled metal spatula shaped rather like a small shovel is ideal for scooping and tossing food in a wok. Alternatively, any good long-handled spoon can be used.

Rack

When steaming food in your wok, you will need a wooden or metal rack or trivet to raise the food above the water level. Wok sets usually include a rack but, if not, Asian and Chinese shops sell them separately. Department stores and hardware shops also sell wooden and metal stands, which can serve the same purpose. Any rack, improvised or not, that keeps the food above the water so that it is steamed and not boiled will suffice.

Bamboo brush

This bundle of stiff, split bamboo is used for cleaning a wok without scrubbing away the seasoned surface. It is an attractive, inexpensive implement but not essential. A soft washing-up brush will do just as well.

Chopping board

One decided improvement over the traditional cooking implements of Asia is the modern chopping board made of hardwood or white acrylic. The typical chopping board is made of soft wood, which is difficult to maintain and, being soft, provides a fertile surface for bacteria. Hardwood or white acrylic boards are easy to clean, resist bacterial accumulation and last much longer.

Asian cooking entails much chopping, slicing and dicing, so it is essential to have a large, steady chopping board. For reasons of hygiene, never place cooked meat on a board on which raw meat or poultry has been prepared. For raw meat, always use a separate board and clean it thoroughly after each use.

Chopsticks

It may come as a surprise to discover that, although the Vietnamese and Singaporeans eat with chopsticks, Indonesians and Malaysians prefer to use forks and spoons. However, you may enjoy serving Asian food with chopsticks. Many Western diners find them a challenge but

Above: bamboo steamers

I always encourage their use. Attempting any new technique is an interesting experience, and chopsticks do indeed offer the novice a physical entrée into many Asian cuisines – a hands-on experience, if you will.

Chopsticks can also be used for stirring, beating, whipping and mixing. But, of course, you can get along nicely with Western spoons, forks, ladles, spatulas and whisks.

Chopsticks are cheap and readily available. I prefer the wooden ones, but in China plastic ones are more commonly used (and re-used) for hygienic and economic reasons.

Cleaver

To cooks of the Far East, the cleaver is an all-purpose cutting instrument that makes all other knives redundant. Once you acquire some skill with a cleaver, you will see how it can be used on all types of food to slice, dice, chop, fillet, shred, crush or whatever. Most Asian chefs rely upon three different sizes of cleaver – light, medium and heavy – to be used as appropriate. Of course, you may use your own familiar kitchen knives instead, but if you decide to invest in a cleaver, choose a good-quality stainless steel model and keep it sharpened.

Deep-fat fryer

A deep-fat fryer is very useful and you may find it safer and easier to use for deep-frying than a wok. The quantities of oil given in the recipes in this book are based on the amount required for deep-frying in a wok. If you are using a deep-fat fryer instead, you will need about double that amount, but never fill it more than half full with oil.

Rice cooker

Electric rice cookers are increasing in popularity. They cook rice perfectly and keep it warm throughout the meal. They also have the advantage of freeing a burner or electric element, so the hob is less cluttered. They are relatively expensive, however, so are only worth buying if you eat rice frequently.

Steamer

Steaming is not a very popular cooking method in the West. This is unfortunate because it is the best way of preparing many foods with a delicate taste and texture, such as fish and vegetables. In the Far East, bamboo steamers have been in use for many centuries. They come in several sizes, of which the 25 cm (10 in) one is the most suitable for home use. The food is placed in the steamer, which is then placed above boiling water in a wok or pot. To stop the food sticking to the steamer as it cooks, put it on a layer of clean, damp muslin. A tight-fitting bamboo lid prevents the steam escaping; several steamers, stacked one above the other, may be used simultaneously.

Before using a bamboo steamer for the first time, wash it and then steam it empty for about 5 minutes. Of course, any kind of wide metal steamer may be used if you prefer.

Miscellaneous

Stainless steel bowls of different sizes, along with sieves and colanders, complete the list of basic implements. They are very useful because you will often have to drain or strain oils and juices and because you will be doing much mixing of wonderful foods. It is better to have one too many tools than one too few.

Conversion tables

Conversions are approximate and have been rounded up or down. Follow one set of measurements only – do not mix metric and Imperial.

Weights		Volume		Measurements	
Metric	**Imperial**	**Metric**	**Imperial**	**Metric**	**Imperial**
15 g	½ oz	25 ml	1 fl oz	0.5 cm	¼ inch
25 g	1 oz	50 ml	2 fl oz	1 cm	½ inch
40 g	1½ oz	85 ml	3 fl oz	2.5 cm	1 inch
50 g	2 oz	150 ml	5 fl oz (¼ pint)	5 cm	2 inches
75 g	3 oz	300 ml	10 fl oz (½ pint)	7.5 cm	3 inches
100 g	4 oz	450 ml	15 fl oz (¾ pint)	10 cm	4 inches
150 g	5 oz	600 ml	1 pint	15 cm	6 inches
175 g	6 oz	700 ml	1¼ pints	18 cm	7 inches
200 g	7 oz	900 ml	1½ pints	20 cm	8 inches
225 g	8 oz	1 litres	1¾ pints	23 cm	9 inches
250 g	9 oz	1.2 litres	2 pints	25 cm	10 inches
275 g	10 oz	1.25 litres	2¼ pints	30 cm	12 inches
350 g	12 oz	1.5 litres	2½ pints		

Weights		Volume		Oven temperatures		
375 g	13 oz	1.6 litres	2¾ pints			
400 g	14 oz	1.75 litres	3 pints	140°C	275°F	Gas Mk 1
425 g	15 oz	1.8 litres	3¼ pints	150°C	300°F	Gas Mk 2
450 g	1 lb	2 litres	3½ pints	160°C	325°F	Gas Mk 3
550 g	1¼ lb	2.1 litres	3¾ pints	180°C	350°F	Gas Mk 4
675 g	1½ lb	2.25 litres	4 pints	190°C	375°F	Gas Mk 5
900 g	2 lb	2.75 litres	5 pints	200°C	400°F	Gas Mk 6
1.5 kg	3 lb	3.4 litres	6 pints	220°C	425°F	Gas Mk 7
1.75 kg	4 lb	3.9 litres	7 pints	230°C	450°F	Gas Mk 8
2.25 kg	5 lb	5 litres	8 pints (1 gal)	240°C	475°F	Gas Mk 9

SOUPS and STARTERS

Vietnamese beef and spinach soup

This Vietnamese soup is similar to one I grew up with in our Chinese household. We used a variety of water spinach with a crisp stalk and distinctive flavour. I have found, however, that ordinary spinach works just as well. This light soup is typical of the subtle cuisine of Vietnam. It is easy to make, and many of the steps can be done in advance.

serves 4
preparation time: 30 minutes
cooking time: 5 minutes

450 g (1 lb) fresh spinach

175 g (6 oz) lean fillet steak, cut into thin slices about 5 cm (2 in) long

2 shallots, finely sliced

2 tablespoons finely chopped garlic

3 tablespoons fish sauce

1.2 litres (2 pints) home-made chicken stock or good-quality bought stock

1 tablespoon lemon juice

1 teaspoon sugar

1 small, fresh red chilli, seeded and chopped

Freshly ground black pepper

1 Remove the stalks from the spinach and wash the leaves well. Blanch the leaves for a few seconds in a large pan of boiling water until they are just wilted. Then drain well and refresh in cold water to prevent further cooking. Drain again, squeezing out excess water.

2 Combine the steak with the shallots, garlic, 1 tablespoon of the fish sauce and some freshly ground black pepper, then set aside. (The soup can be prepared in advance up to this point.)

4 Add the blanched spinach and stir in the beef and its marinade. Bring the soup back to simmering point, add a few grindings of freshly ground black pepper to taste and serve at once.

3 Just before you are ready to eat, bring the chicken stock to a simmer in a saucepan and season it with the remaining fish sauce, the lemon juice, sugar and chilli.

Vietnamese soup with beancurd

This hearty, colourful soup is light and healthy, yet is almost a meal in itself. I am reminded how similar it is to many of the soups from southern China. Easy to make, it relies on good chicken stock for its success.

serves 4
preparation time: 25 minutes, plus 10 minutes' marinating
cooking time: 5 minutes

100 g (4 oz) lean, boneless pork chops, cut into thin slices 5 cm (2 in) long

100 g (4 oz) raw prawns, shelled and de-veined (see pages 16–17)

5 teaspoons fish sauce

2 tablespoons chopped spring onions (white part only)

450 g (1 lb) silken or firm beancurd

1.2 litres (2 pints) home-made chicken stock or good-quality bought stock

Salt and freshly ground black pepper

To garnish:

3 tablespoons chopped fresh chives

2 fresh red chillies, seeded and chopped

1 In a bowl, combine the pork, prawns, 2 teaspoons of the fish sauce and the spring onions. Leave to marinate for 10 minutes.

2 Gently cut the beancurd into 1 cm (½ in) cubes and leave to drain on kitchen paper for 10 minutes.

3 Pour the chicken stock into a saucepan and bring to a simmer. Add the marinated prawn and pork mixture and simmer for 2 minutes.

4 Add the beancurd and the remaining fish sauce and simmer for another 2 minutes. Season to taste with salt and pepper, then remove from the heat, garnish with the chives and chillies and serve.

Indonesian-style chicken soup

Many years ago, when I was in Jakarta, a brilliant cook hosted a wonderful buffet consisting of all the regional dishes of Indonesia. This spicy soup was one of my favourites. It relies on really good chicken stock for its success, and makes a zesty starter for any meal.

serves 4
preparation time: 40 minutes
cooking time: 25 minutes

100 g (4 oz) fresh or dried egg noodles

1 teaspoon sesame oil

3 tablespoons groundnut oil

6 garlic cloves, finely sliced

6 shallots, finely sliced

2 teaspoons shrimp paste

1 teaspoon ground turmeric

1 tablespoon ground coriander

2 teaspoons ground cumin

2 teaspoons salt

2 fresh red or green chillies, seeded and finely shredded

1.2 litres (2 pints) home-made chicken stock or good-quality bought stock

2 teaspoons lemon juice

Freshly ground black pepper

To garnish:

2 spring onions, finely shredded

2 eggs, hard-boiled for 10 minutes, then shelled and quartered

Prawn crackers

1 lime, cut into eighths

1 Cook the noodles for 3–5 minutes in a pan of boiling water, until tender. Drain and plunge them into cold water. Drain again thoroughly and toss them with the sesame oil, then set aside.

2 Heat a wok or large frying-pan over a high heat. Add the groundnut oil and, when it is very hot and slightly smoking, add the garlic and shallots. Stir-fry them until they are crisp and golden brown. Remove with a slotted spoon, drain on kitchen paper and set aside.

3 Now add the shrimp paste, turmeric, coriander, cumin, salt, chillies and some freshly ground black pepper to the wok and stir-fry for 1 minute.

4 Add the stock, turn the heat to low, then cover and simmer for 10 minutes. Stir in the lemon juice and simmer for 2 minutes. Ladle into a large soup tureen, add the cooked noodles and serve at once with the garnishes, including the fried garlic and shallots, in separate bowls.

Crispy Vietnamese spring rolls

This is perhaps one of the tastiest versions of spring rolls in all of Asia. Crackling rice paper skins are rolled round a savoury filling, eaten in a leaf of fresh lettuce with herb sprigs and dipped in a spicy sauce. I think you will find it tasty and fun to eat. The sauce can be made well ahead of time. Although the rolls can be made in advance, too, it is best to deep-fry them at the last minute. They are terrific treats to serve with drinks or as a lovely first course for a dinner party.

The rice paper wrappers can be found in Chinese or Southeast Asian grocery shops. Handle them with care, as they are quite fragile. You will see, however, that such care is well repaid by the pleasure that this delicate treat affords.

> makes about 25 small spring rolls
> preparation time: 1 hour, plus 20 minutes' soaking
> cooking time: about 25 minutes

1 packet of 15 cm (6 in) round rice paper wrappers

5 tablespoons plain flour, mixed with 6 tablespoons cold water

400 ml (14 fl oz) oil, preferably groundnut oil

225 g (8 oz) iceberg lettuce, leaves separated

Assorted sprigs of fresh basil, mint or coriander, or all 3

For the filling:

25 g (1 oz) bean-thread (transparent) noodles

10 g (¼ oz) dried wood ear fungus or Chinese dried mushrooms

1 tablespoon groundnut oil

1 small onion, finely chopped

2 tablespoons coarsely chopped garlic

2 tablespoons finely chopped spring onions

2 tablespoons finely chopped shallots

225 g (8 oz) minced pork

1½ teaspoons salt

½ teaspoon freshly ground black pepper

100 g (4 oz) cooked fresh crab meat

For the dipping sauce (*nuoc cham*):

2 tablespoons fish sauce

1–2 fresh red chillies, seeded and chopped

1 tablespoon finely chopped garlic

1 tablespoon lime or lemon juice

4 tablespoons water

1 tablespoon sugar

1 For the filling, soak the noodles in a large bowl of warm water for 15 minutes. When they are soft, drain them and cut into 7.5 cm (3 in) lengths, using scissors or a knife.

2 Soak the wood ears or Chinese mushrooms in warm water for about 20 minutes, until soft. Rinse well in cold water and squeeze out the excess liquid. Remove any hard stalks and finely shred the mushrooms.

3 While the mushrooms are soaking, make the dipping sauce. Combine all the ingredients in a blender, processing them thoroughly. Pour into a small bowl and leave to stand for at least 10 minutes before using.

4 Heat a wok or large frying-pan over a high heat. Add the groundnut oil for the filling and, when it is very hot and slightly smoking, add the onion, garlic, spring onions and shallots and stir-fry for 3 minutes. Then add the pork, salt and pepper and continue to stir-fry for 5 minutes. Drain the mixture in a colander and leave to cool.

5 Combine the mixture in a large bowl with the bean-thread noodles, mushrooms and crab meat.

6 To make the spring rolls, fill a large bowl with warm water. Dip one of the rice paper rounds in the water and let it soften, then remove and drain on a tea-towel. Transfer the softened rice paper wrapper to a board, put about 2 tablespoons of the filling on it, then fold in each side and roll it up tightly.

7 Seal the ends with a little of the flour paste. You should have a roll about 7.5 cm (3 in) long, a little like a small sausage. Repeat the procedure until you have used up all the filling.

8 Heat the oil in a deep-fat fryer or a large wok. Deep-fry the spring rolls until they are golden brown. They have a tendency to stick to each other at the beginning of frying, so fry only a few at a time. Do not attempt to break them apart should they stick together. You can do this after they have been removed from the oil. Drain them on kitchen paper and serve at once, with the lettuce leaves, herb sprigs and the dipping sauce.

Grilled Indonesian prawn skewers

One of the pleasures of walking through the streets of Jakarta is smelling the wafting aromas of the various grilled foods being cooked. This dish is probably one of my favourites – juicy, succulent prawns that have been marinated and then cooked quickly on a barbecue or hot grill. The smoky chargrill taste complements the delicious prawns so well. This dish takes only minutes to cook.

serves 4–6
preparation time: 30 minutes, plus at least 1 hour's marinating
cooking time: 4–6 minutes

450 g (1 lb) raw prawns, shelled and de-veined (see pages 16–17)

For the marinade:
120 ml (4 fl oz) canned coconut milk
1 teaspoon salt

½ teaspoon freshly ground black pepper
1 tablespoon fish sauce
3 tablespoons lime juice
2 tablespoons finely chopped garlic
1 teaspoon finely chopped lime zest

2 small, fresh red chillies, seeded and chopped
2 teaspoons sugar
1 teaspoon shrimp paste

1 Soak 12 bamboo skewers in cold water for 15 minutes. Meanwhile, combine all the marinade ingredients in a large bowl and mix well.

2 Add the prawns to the marinade and mix well. Cover with cling film and leave to marinate in the fridge for at least 1 hour.

3 When you are ready to barbecue the prawns, remove them from the marinade and thread 1 or 2 on each bamboo skewer. Reserve the marinade.

4 Prepare a barbecue or preheat a ridged chargrill pan or the oven grill. When the charcoal is ash white or the grill is very hot, grill the prawn skewers for 2–3 minutes on each side, until they are cooked through.

5 Pour the marinade into a small saucepan and simmer for 2 minutes. Arrange the prawn skewers on a warm platter and serve immediately, accompanied by the sauce.

Indonesian vegetable salad

This is a delightful cooked vegetarian salad, dressed with a bold peanut sauce. Considered a national dish in Indonesia, it makes the perfect antidote to the hot, humid weather of Java. I find it makes a good light first course for a dinner party, or it can be served as a meal in itself.

serves 4
preparation time: 45 minutes
cooking time: 10 minutes

225 g (8 oz) carrots, peeled and thinly sliced

100 g (4 oz) small broccoli florets

100 g (4 oz) small cauliflower florets

100 g (4 oz) green beans, trimmed

100 g (4 oz) fresh bean sprouts, rinsed

3 tablespoons groundnut oil

5 shallots, sliced

1 quantity of Peanut Dipping Sauce (see pages 46–7)

Salt and freshly ground black pepper

To garnish:

2 eggs, hard-boiled for 10–12 minutes, then shelled and cut into quarters

Prawn crackers

1 small cucumber, thinly sliced

1 Bring a large pan of salted water to the boil. Add the carrots, broccoli, cauliflower and green beans and cook for 3 minutes, then add the bean sprouts and cook for 1 minute. Drain the vegetables, place in a warm bowl and season with salt and pepper.

2 Heat a wok, then add the groundnut oil. When the oil is hot, toss in the sliced shallots and fry slowly until crisp and brown (watch them carefully so they don't burn). Remove immediately with a slotted spoon and drain on kitchen paper.

3 Drizzle the peanut sauce over the vegetables and mix well, then transfer to a serving platter. Garnish with the fried shallots, arrange the rest of the garnishes on top and serve at once.

Vietnamese prawn paste skewers

This delightful appetizer is known in Vietnamese as *chao tom*. It can be made well in advance and grilled at the last moment, making it an ideal starter as well as a very original one. You can substitute thick bamboo skewers for sugar cane, soaking them in cold water for 15 minutes before use.

serves 4
preparation time: 1 hour
cooking time: 10 minutes

Sesame oil

1 or 2 pieces of fresh sugar cane, cut into about ten 7.5 cm (3 in) lengths

225 g (8 oz) iceberg lettuce, leaves separated

Assorted sprigs of fresh basil, mint or coriander, or all 3

1 quantity of Dipping Sauce (*nuoc cham*, see page 34)

For the prawn paste:

450 g (1 lb) raw prawns, shelled and de-veined (see pages 16–17)

100 g (4 oz) minced fatty pork

1 teaspoon salt

1/2 teaspoon freshly ground black pepper

1 egg white

2 tablespoons finely chopped spring onions (white part only)

2 tablespoons finely chopped garlic

1 teaspoon finely chopped fresh ginger

1 teaspoon cornflour (more if needed)

2 teaspoons sugar

1 teaspoon fish sauce

1 Using a cleaver or a large, sharp knife, chop the prawns coarsely and then mince them finely into a paste. Transfer to a bowl and mix in the rest of the ingredients for the prawn paste, adding a little more cornflour if the mixture is too moist (alternatively, you could do all this in a food processor). This step can be done several hours in advance, but you should then wrap the paste well in cling film and put it in the refrigerator until you need it.

2 Lightly oil your hands with sesame oil. Take about 2 tablespoons of the prawn paste and wrap it evenly around a length of sugar cane, leaving about 1 cm (1/2 in) exposed at each end. Repeat with the remaining prawn paste and sugar cane. You should have around 10 pieces.

3 Next set up a steamer, or put a rack into a wok or deep saucepan and fill it with 5 cm (2 in) of water. Bring the water to the boil over a high heat. Put the prawn pieces on a heatproof plate and then carefully lower it into the steamer or on to the rack. Turn the heat to low and cover the wok or pan tightly. Steam gently for 3 minutes. The prawn skewers can be made in advance up to this point.

4 When you are ready to serve the skewers, prepare a barbecue or preheat a ridged chargrill pan or the oven grill. When the charcoal is ash white or the grill is very hot, grill the prawns for 3 minutes on each side. Put the cooked skewers on a warm platter and serve immediately. To eat, remove the prawn paste from the cane, wrap in a lettuce leaf with a few sprigs of herbs and dip into the sauce. Of course, one can always chew on the sugar cane.

Malaysian prawn fritters

I remember the first time I had these fritters at a roadside restaurant in Kuala Lumpur. Quickly fried and served immediately, they were absolutely divine. Then I discovered how easy they were to make. They make a wonderful first course with salad, or serve them with drinks.

makes about 20
preparation time: 40 minutes
cooking time: about 10 minutes

450 g (1 lb) raw prawns, shelled and de-veined (see pages 16–17)

225 g (8 oz) fresh bean sprouts, rinsed

120 g (4$1/2$ oz) plain flour

2 teaspoons baking powder

2 small, fresh red chillies, seeded and finely chopped

1 teaspoon ground coriander

$1/2$ teaspoon ground turmeric

2 tablespoons finely chopped spring onions

2 tablespoons finely chopped fresh coriander

1 teaspoon salt

2 eggs, beaten

400 ml (14 fl oz) oil, preferably groundnut, for deep-frying

Freshly ground black pepper

1 Finely chop half the prawns. Combine the chopped prawns with the bean sprouts, flour, baking powder, chillies, ground coriander, turmeric, spring onions, fresh coriander, salt, pepper and eggs. Mix well.

2 Take a dessertspoonful of the chopped mixture, place one whole prawn on top and press it into the mixture so that the prawn is set in. Continue until you have used up all the mixture and whole prawns.

3 Heat the oil in a deep-fat fryer or a large wok. Deep-fry the fritters, a few at a time, for 2–3 minutes, until they are golden brown. Drain them on kitchen paper and serve at once.

Fresh Vietnamese spring rolls

I love these unusual, sparkling-fresh spring rolls. They make a perfect starter and I have often served them as a main course, especially on hot, humid summer evenings. The great advantage is that they can be made several hours in advance. You can buy rice paper wrappers in Chinese or Thai food shops.

serves 4–8
preparation time: 50 minutes, plus 15 minutes' soaking
cooking time: 3 minutes

350 g (12 oz) raw prawns, shelled and de-veined (see pages 16–17)

50 g (2 oz) bean-thread (transparent) noodles

225 g (8 oz) soft salad leaves

Large bunches of fresh basil, mint and coriander

1 packet of 20 cm (8 in) round rice paper wrappers

225 g (8 oz) fresh bean sprouts, rinsed

For the peanut dipping sauce:

2 tablespoons fish sauce

1–2 fresh red chillies, seeded and chopped

1 tablespoon finely chopped garlic

2 tablespoons lime or lemon juice

5 tablespoons water

1 tablespoon sugar

3 tablespoons roasted peanuts, crushed

1 First make the peanut dipping sauce. Combine all the ingredients except the peanuts in a blender and process thoroughly. Pour into a small bowl and leave to stand for at least 10 minutes before using (the sauce can be prepared several hours in advance, if necessary).

2 Blanch the prawns in a pan of boiling salted water for 3 minutes, drain well and then cut them in half lengthways. Set aside.

3 Soak the noodles in a large bowl of hot water for 15 minutes, until soft, then drain. Cut them into 7.5 cm (3 in) lengths, using scissors or a knife. Wash the salad leaves well and spin them dry in a salad spinner. Do the same with the basil, mint and coriander.

4 When you are ready to make the spring rolls, fill a large bowl with warm water. Dip one of the rice paper rounds in the water and let it soften, then remove and drain on a tea-towel. Put a large salad leaf on the softened rice paper wrapper. Add a spoonful of the noodles to the salad leaf, then add 3 basil leaves and 3 mint leaves. Then carefully roll the rice paper halfway up.

5 Now place 3 pieces of prawn, 3 coriander sprigs and 2 tablespoons of bean sprouts on the wrapper. Fold the 2 ends in, then keep rolling until the entire rice paper is rolled up. Repeat with all the remaining ingredients. Cover the spring rolls with a damp tea-towel until you are ready to serve them (do not refrigerate; they are meant to be served at room temperature). Just before serving, stir the crushed peanuts into the sauce. Cut each spring roll in half on the diagonal and serve with the sauce.

Warm Vietnamese beef salad

This is one of my favourite Vietnamese dishes. It has a clean, light flavour, with the stir-fried beef paired with a freshly dressed green salad that is typical of dishes served in tropical Vietnam. Although it is often served as a starter, I find it equally delicious as a main course in hot weather; simply double the quantities or add more salad.

serves 4–6
preparation time: 20 minutes, plus 20 minutes' marinating
cooking time: 3 minutes

450 g (1 lb) lean, tender beef fillet

1 tablespoon fish sauce

1 tablespoon light soy sauce

1 teaspoon sugar

3 tablespoons oil, preferably groundnut oil

5 tablespoons coarsely chopped garlic

225 g (8 oz) soft salad leaves

For the dressing:

3 tablespoons white rice vinegar

1 tablespoon finely chopped garlic

2 teaspoons sesame oil

3 tablespoons oil, preferably groundnut oil

6 tablespoons finely sliced shallots

Salt and freshly ground black pepper

1 First make the dressing. In a large salad bowl, combine the vinegar, garlic and some salt and pepper. Gradually beat in the sesame and groundnut oils, then stir in the shallots and set aside.

2 Cut the beef into slices 5 cm (2 in) long and 5 mm (1/4 in) thick, slicing against the grain of the meat. Put the beef into a bowl together with the fish sauce, soy sauce, sugar and some black pepper. Mix well and then leave to marinate for about 20 minutes.

3 Heat a wok or large frying-pan over a high heat until it is very hot. Add the oil and, when it is hot, add the garlic and stir-fry for 20 seconds, until golden brown. Remove with a slotted spoon and drain on kitchen paper.

4 Reheat the oil and, when it is very hot and slightly smoking, add the beef to the wok and stir-fry for 2 minutes, until it is barely cooked. Remove it and leave to drain in a colander or sieve.

5 Add the greens to the dressing in the salad bowl and toss thoroughly. Arrange on a serving platter, garnish with the browned garlic and top with the warm beef. Serve at once.

FISH and SHELLFISH

Balinese-style crispy fish

One of the culinary delights of visiting Bali is their wonderful array of fish dishes. Here is a simple one that I love. It is quick and easy to make but embodies all the tastes of the tropics. Once the sauce is made, all that is left to do is fry the fish, which takes literally minutes.

serves 2–4
preparation time: 20 minutes
cooking time: 15 minutes

1 teaspoon salt
1/2 teaspoon freshly ground
  black pepper
450 g (1 lb) white flat-fish
  fillets, such as Dover sole or
  plaice, skinned
Cornflour for dusting
6 tablespoons groundnut oil

For the sauce:
2 tablespoons groundnut oil
2 onions, finely chopped
3 tablespoons finely chopped
  garlic
2 teaspoons finely chopped
  fresh ginger
1 teaspoon grated lemon zest
1 teaspoon salt
1 tablespoon dark soy sauce
2 tablespoons lemon juice
Freshly ground black pepper

1 First make the sauce. Heat a wok or large frying-pan over a high heat. Add the oil and, when it is very hot and slightly smoking, add the onions. Stir-fry for 5 minutes or until they are soft and translucent.

2 Add the garlic, ginger, lemon zest, salt, soy sauce, lemon juice and some black pepper. Reduce the heat to low and simmer for 2 minutes, then set aside.

3 Sprinkle the salt and pepper evenly over the fish fillets and dust them with cornflour, shaking off any excess.

5 Turn over and brown the other side. Remove the fish and drain on kitchen paper, then transfer to a warm platter. Repeat with the remaining oil and fish. Spoon the sauce over the fish and serve at once.

4 You will need to cook the fish in 2 batches. Heat a wok, add half the oil and, when it is very hot, add half the fish. Fry for 2 minutes, until it is crisp and brown underneath.

Malaysian fish curry

I have eaten this wonderfully fragrant curry many times in Malaysia, where fresh fish is a standard item in every home and on every restaurant menu. It makes an ideal quick meal. This savoury, delectable treat goes perfectly with plain rice.

serves 2–4
preparation time: 20 minutes
cooking time: 10 minutes

450 g (1 lb) firm white fish fillets, such as cod, halibut or sea bass, skinned

For the curry paste:
175 g (6 oz) onions, coarsely chopped

1 1/2 tablespoons finely chopped fresh ginger

1 tablespoon finely chopped garlic

2 tablespoons Madras curry paste

1 teaspoon ground coriander

1/2 teaspoon ground fennel seeds

1/2 teaspoon ground turmeric

2 tablespoons lemon juice

150 ml (5 fl oz) canned coconut milk

1 Cut the fish into 5 cm (2 in) pieces and set aside.

2 For the curry paste, put the onions, ginger, garlic, curry paste, coriander, fennel, turmeric and lemon juice in a food processor. Add half the coconut milk and blend very well.

3 Pour the remaining coconut milk into a wok or saucepan and add the curry paste. Bring the mixture to a simmer and cook for 5 minutes. Add the fish pieces and cook for 5 minutes longer. Serve at once.

Singapore-style steamed fish

One of the highlights of eating in Singapore is tasting Nonya cuisine. This fantastic and intriguing cooking style comes from the Babas, a mixture of ethnic Chinese and Malays – one of the first fusion cuisines, if you like. Many of the dishes combine Chinese subtlety with the assertive flavours of Malaysian cooking. Here is one example of their many contributions. Only the freshest fish will do.

serves 4
preparation time: 15 minutes,
 plus 20 minutes' soaking
cooking time: 5–14 minutes

450 g (1 lb) firm white fish
   fillets, such as cod or
   sole, or 1 whole fish such as
   sole or turbot, weighing
   675–900 g (1¹/₂–2 lb)

1 teaspoon coarse sea salt or
   plain salt

15 g (¹/₂ oz) Chinese dried
   mushrooms

3 tablespoons Chinese
   preserved vegetables

2 tablespoons light soy sauce

Freshly ground black pepper

To garnish:

A handful of fresh coriander
   sprigs

3 tablespoons finely
   shredded spring onions

1 Pat the fish fillets or whole fish dry with kitchen paper. Rub evenly with the salt and some pepper (on the outside as well as the inside if you are using a whole fish), then set aside.

2 Soak the mushrooms in warm water for 20 minutes, then drain and squeeze out excess liquid. Remove and discard the stalks and finely shred the caps into thin strips. Soak the Chinese preserved vegetables in water for 10 minutes to remove some of the salt, then drain and finely shred them.

4 Put the plate of fish into the steamer or on to the rack. Cover the pan tightly and gently steam the fish until it is just cooked. Flat fish fillets will take about 5 minutes to cook; whole fish or fillets such as sea bass will take 12–14 minutes. When it is done, the fish will turn opaque and flake slightly but should still remain moist. Remove the plate of cooked fish and scatter the coriander and spring onions on top. Serve at once.

3 Next set up a steamer, or put a rack into a wok or deep pan and fill it with 5 cm (2 in) of water. Bring the water to the boil over a high heat. Put the fish on a heatproof plate and scatter the mushrooms and preserved vegetables evenly over the top. Sprinkle the soy sauce over all.

Malaysian black bean fish

When I first tasted this dish during a visit to Malaysia, I immediately recognized the Chinese influence. However, it had a pungency that was uniquely Malay. Now I often make this tasty, light and satisfying dish, which is the hallmark of the best Malaysian home cooking.

serves 4

preparation time: 25 minutes, plus 20 minutes' standing

cooking time: 10 minutes

450 g (1 lb) firm white fish fillets, such as cod, halibut or sea bass, skinned

2 teaspoons salt

3 tablespoons groundnut oil

3 tablespoons finely shredded spring onions

For the sauce:

1 tablespoon groundnut oil

1½ tablespoons coarsely chopped salted black beans

2 tablespoons finely chopped garlic

2 teaspoons finely chopped fresh ginger

1 small onion, chopped

3 fresh green chillies, seeded and chopped

225 g (8 oz) button mushrooms, sliced

3 tablespoons finely chopped spring onions

1 tablespoon light soy sauce

1 tablespoon lemon juice

1 teaspoon sugar

½ teaspoon salt

1 teaspoon freshly ground black pepper

1 Cut the fish fillets into strips 2.5 cm (1 in) wide and sprinkle the salt evenly over them. Leave for 20 minutes.

2 Heat a wok or large frying-pan over a high heat. Add the oil and, when it is very hot and slightly smoking, turn the heat down to medium and add the fish strips. Fry these gently for about 2 minutes or until they are brown on both sides, taking care not to break them up. Remove with a slotted spoon and drain on kitchen paper. Drain off most of the oil from the wok, leaving about 1½ table-spoons.

3 Reheat the wok, add the groundnut oil for the sauce, plus the black beans, garlic, ginger and onion, and stir-fry for 2 minutes. Then add the chillies, button mushrooms and spring onions and continue to stir-fry for 3 minutes over a high heat.

4 Now add the soy sauce, lemon juice, sugar, salt and pepper. Stir-fry for 10 seconds. Return the fish to the wok and gently finish cooking it in the sauce for about 1 minute. Give the mixture a good stir. Using a slotted spoon, arrange the fish on a warm serving platter, garnish with the spring onions and serve at once.

very good

Hot and sour Indonesian prawns

Seafood is a staple of the Indonesian diet. This simple but delectable dish is typical of the cooking found in many homes. Prawns cook quickly, so they make ideal fast food. Serve with plain rice for a complete meal.

serves 4
preparation time: 25 minutes
cooking time: 10 minutes

1½ tablespoons groundnut oil

1 small onion, chopped

1 tablespoon finely chopped garlic

2 teaspoons finely chopped fresh ginger

2 fresh red chillies, seeded and chopped

1 teaspoon ground cumin

1 teaspoon ground coriander

1 teaspoon shrimp paste

1 teaspoon sugar

450 g (1 lb) raw prawns, shelled and de-veined (see pages 16–17)

3 tablespoons lemon juice

1 Heat a wok or large frying-pan over a high heat. Add the oil and, when it is very hot and slightly smoking, add the onion, garlic, ginger and chillies and stir-fry for 3 minutes.

2 Add the cumin, coriander and shrimp paste and stir-fry for 1 minute.

3 Now add the sugar and prawns and stir-fry for 2 minutes. Add the lemon juice, turn the heat down and simmer for 4 minutes or until most of the liquid has evaporated. Serve immediately.

Crispy Vietnamese prawns

This simple but tasty recipe makes a delightful main course or starter. With its subtlety and ease, it bears all the hallmarks of Vietnamese cooking. Much of the work can be done in advance. However, for crispy, succulent prawns, the frying should be left until the last moment.

serves 4
preparation time: 40 minutes, plus 1 hour's marinating
cooking time: about 15 minutes

450 g (1 lb) raw prawns, shelled and de-veined (see pages 16–17)

1 tablespoon fish sauce

3 tablespoons finely chopped garlic

1/2 teaspoon freshly ground black pepper

Cornflour for dusting

600 ml (1 pint) groundnut or vegetable oil, for deep-frying

For the batter:

150 g (5 oz) plain flour

2 tablespoons baking powder

1 teaspoon sugar

1/2 teaspoon ground turmeric

1/2 teaspoon salt

300 ml (10 fl oz) water

For the sweet and spicy dipping sauce:

150 ml (5 fl oz) water

3 tablespoons sugar

3 tablespoons Chinese white rice vinegar or cider vinegar

3 tablespoons tomato purée or tomato ketchup

2 teaspoons chilli bean sauce

1 teaspoon salt

1/2 teaspoon freshly ground white pepper

1 teaspoon cornflour, mixed with 2 teaspoons water

1 Combine the prawns, fish sauce, garlic and black pepper in a bowl and leave to marinate for 1 hour.

2 In a bowl, combine all the ingredients for the batter. Mix until smooth, then cover and leave to stand for 1 hour.

3 In a small saucepan, combine all the ingredients for the sweet and spicy sauce except the cornflour mixture. Bring to the boil, stir in the cornflour mixture and simmer for 1 minute. Remove from the heat and leave to cool.

4 Dust the prawns with corn-flour, shaking off any excess.

5 Heat a wok or deep-fat fryer. Add the oil and, when it is very hot and slightly smoking, dip a handful of prawns into the batter and deep-fry them for 3 minutes, until crisp and golden. If the oil gets too hot, turn the heat down slightly. Drain the prawns well on kitchen paper and then fry the remaining prawns in the same way. Serve immediately, with the sweet and spicy dipping sauce.

good, but spicy

Fragrant Singapore-style prawn curry

I enjoyed this delightful stir-fry dish for the first time in Singapore some years ago. Prawns have a delicate but distinctive flavour, and the clean, mildly citrus touch of the lemon grass makes a perfect counterpart. The quick cooking style ensures that the two main ingredients remain at their best. Use fresh lemon grass whenever possible – in a dish like this it is worth a detour to obtain it. But if your search is in vain, you could substitute 2 tablespoons of grated lemon zest.

serves 2–4
preparation time: 25 minutes
cooking time: 6 minutes

1 fresh lemon grass stalk

1 fresh red or green chilli

2 tablespoons groundnut oil

100 g (4 oz) onion, coarsely chopped

2 tablespoons finely chopped garlic

2 teaspoons finely chopped fresh ginger

450 g (1 lb) raw prawns, shelled and de-veined (see pages 16–17)

2 teaspoons Madras curry paste

1 teaspoon chilli bean sauce

1 teaspoon sugar

2 tablespoons water

1 tablespoon Shaoxing rice wine or dry sherry

2 teaspoons light soy sauce

1/2 teaspoon salt

1/4 teaspoon freshly ground black pepper

Fresh coriander sprigs or lime wedges, to garnish

1 Peel off the tough outer layers of the lemon grass stalk, leaving the tender, whitish centre. Chop it finely. Cut the chilli in half and carefully remove and discard the seeds. Chop the chilli finely and combine it with the lemon grass.

2 Heat a wok or large frying-pan over a high heat. Add the oil and, when it is very hot and slightly smoking, add the onion, garlic, ginger, lemon grass and chilli and stir-fry for 1 minute. Then add the prawns and stir-fry for 1 minute longer.

3 Now add all the remaining ingredients except the coriander and stir-fry for 4 minutes or until the prawns are firm and cooked. Turn the mixture on to a warm serving platter, garnish with the coriander sprigs and serve at once.

Vietnamese salt and pepper crab

I remember the first time I had this delectable crab dish in a Vietnamese restaurant in Hong Kong, and was thrilled to discover later how easy it is to make. The secret is to use very fresh crabs – preferably live. They are then quickly stir-fried with plenty of salt and freshly ground black pepper. Nothing could be simpler or tastier.

The Vietnamese traditionally eat the crab with their fingers, so I suggest that you have a large finger bowl of water decorated with lemon slices on the table.

serves 4
preparation time: 30 minutes
cooking time: 20 minutes

1 live or freshly cooked crab
   in the shell, weighing about
   1.5 kg (3 lb)
2 tablespoons groundnut oil
6 tablespoons coarsely
   chopped garlic
2 teaspoons salt
1 teaspoon freshly ground
   black pepper

For the dipping sauce:
1 teaspoon salt
Juice and grated zest of
   1 lemon
Freshly ground black pepper

1 To cook a live crab, bring a large pot of water to the boil, add 2 teaspoons of salt and then put in the crab. Cover the pot and cook the crab for about 5–7 minutes, until it turns bright red. Remove with a large slotted spoon and drain in a colander. Leave to cool.

2 Place the cooked crab on its back on a board. Using your fingers, twist the claws from the body. They should come off quite easily.

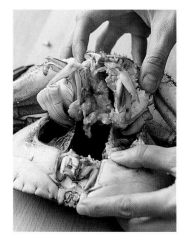

3 Now twist off the bony tail flap on the underside of the crab and discard it. With your fingers, prise the body from the main shell. Remove and discard the small, bag-like stomach sac and its appendages, which are located just behind the crab's mouth.

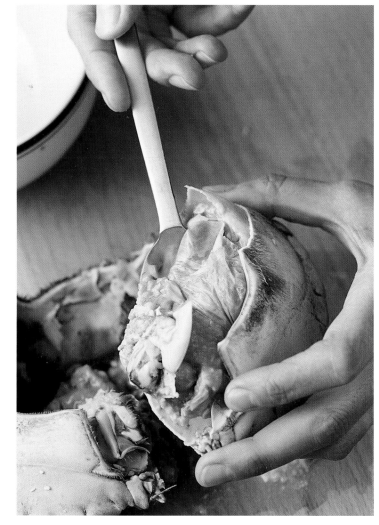

5 Using a cleaver or a heavy knife, split the crab body in half and, using a spoon, fork or skewer, scrape out all the brown and white crabmeat from the body.

4 Pull the soft feathery gills, which look a little like fingers, away from the body and discard them. Remove the legs and put to one side.

6 Using a heavy knife or cleaver, cut the crab, shell included, into large pieces. Crack the claws and legs slightly.

7 Heat a wok or large frying-pan over a high heat. Add the oil and, when it is very hot and slightly smoking, add the garlic and stir-fry for 20–30 seconds, until lightly browned. Then add the crab pieces and crabmeat and stir-fry for 10 minutes. Now add the salt and pepper, mix well and cook for another minute. Turn the crab on to a large, warm serving platter.

8 Combine all the dipping sauce ingredients in a small bowl and serve with the crab.

Singapore-style chilli crab

One of the dishes that all natives insist visitors to Singapore must try is their famous chilli crab. It is a food you eat at street hawkers' stalls, sitting outside and using your fingers — not only is it fun but it is also quite delicious. All the ingredients are thrown into a very hot wok in front of your eyes and in minutes the most fragrant, addictive crab dish emerges. Of course, like all crab dishes, only the freshest crab will do.

The Singaporeans traditionally eat the crab with their fingers, so I suggest that you have a large finger bowl of water decorated with lemon slices on the table.

serves 4
preparation time: 30 minutes
cooking time: 20 minutes

1 live or freshly cooked crab in the shell, weighing about 1.5 kg (3 lb)
2 tablespoons groundnut oil
4 tablespoons coarsely chopped garlic
1 tablespoon finely chopped fresh ginger
3 fresh red chillies, seeded and chopped
6 tablespoons chilli sauce
6 tablespoons tomato passata
1 teaspoon salt

1 Cook and prepare the crab following steps 1–6 of Vietnamese Salt and Pepper Crab (see pages 66–9).

2 Heat a wok or large frying-pan over a high heat. Add the oil and, when it is very hot and slightly smoking, add the garlic and ginger and stir-fry for 20–30 seconds, until lightly browned. Then add the chillies, chilli sauce, tomato passata and salt and mix well.

3 Now add the crab pieces and crabmeat and stir-fry for 10 minutes. Turn the crab on to a large, warm platter and serve immediately.

Singapore-style oyster omelette

This recipe is derived from the ones made by Singapore fish hawkers. It is delicious, flavoursome and satisfying, and prepared right in front of you. That is how I learned how easy it is to make. Sweet potato flour gives it a delightful, slightly chewy texture and quite an unusual flavour. It may be obtained at a Chinese grocer's but if you cannot find it, plain flour can be substituted at a pinch.

Serve this omelette as a main course or as a starter for a special meal.

serves 4
preparation time: 30 minutes
cooking time: 5 minutes

1 dozen oysters

100 g (4 oz) sweet potato flour

450 ml (15 fl oz) water

2 teaspoons salt

2 teaspoons Shaoxing rice wine or dry sherry

4 eggs, beaten

2 tablespoons groundnut oil

3 tablespoons finely chopped garlic

3 tablespoons finely chopped spring onions

1½ tablespoons chilli bean sauce

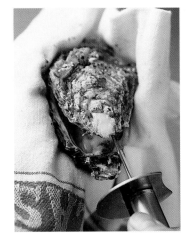

1 To open the oysters, cover one hand with a thick cloth and hold an oyster in it. Using a short, sharp, heavy knife in the other hand, prise the shell open next to the hinge. Cut the muscle to loosen the oyster from the shell. Tip the oyster and its juices into a colander set over a bowl. Repeat with the remaining oysters, reserving the juices. Pat the oysters dry with kitchen paper.

2 Make a batter by mixing the sweet potato flour with the water, salt, rice wine or sherry and the reserved oyster juices, then beat in the eggs until smooth.

5 Reduce the heat and cook for another 3 minutes, until the egg has set. Serve at once, cut into wedges.

3 Heat a wok or large frying-pan over a high heat. Add the oil and, when it is very hot and slightly smoking, pour in the egg mixture. Stir quickly for 30 seconds.

4 Then add the garlic, spring onions, chilli bean sauce and oysters and stir-fry for 1 minute.

MEAT and POULTRY

Vietnamese-style beef stew

In some ways, this Vietnamese version of beef stew is similar to the classic Chinese one. Yet the use of aromatic lemon grass gives it a distinctive Vietnamese touch, as does the fragrant garnish of basil and mint. Be sure to use an inexpensive cut of beef, such as brisket or shin. This hearty but very tasty dish is perfect for a cold winter's night. Plain steamed rice is the most natural accompaniment.

serves 4–6
preparation time: 45 minutes
cooking time: 2³/4–3¹/4 hours

6 fresh lemon grass stalks

2 tablespoons groundnut oil

1.5 kg (3 lb) stewing beef, such as brisket or shin, cut into 5 cm (2 in) cubes

4 spring onions, cut on a slight diagonal into 5 cm (2 in) lengths

1 small onion, coarsely chopped

6 slices of fresh ginger

6 garlic cloves, lightly crushed

2–3 teaspoons crushed dried red chilli

450 g (1 lb) carrots, peeled and cut on a slight diagonal into 5 cm (2 in) chunks

For the braising sauce:

900 ml (1¹/2 pints) home-made chicken stock or good-quality bought stock

75 g (3 oz) rock sugar or granulated sugar

3 tablespoons light soy sauce

2 tablespoons dark soy sauce

3 tablespoons Shaoxing rice wine or dry sherry

4 star anise

2 teaspoons five-spice powder

2 tablespoons tomato purée

2 teaspoons salt

1 teaspoon freshly ground black pepper

To garnish:

6 tablespoons coarsely chopped fresh basil

2 tablespoons coarsely chopped fresh mint

1 Peel off the tough outer layers of the lemon grass stalks, leaving the tender, whitish centre. Crush with the flat of a knife, then cut into 7.5 cm (3 in) pieces.

2 Heat a wok or large frying-pan, add the oil and, when it is very hot and slightly smoking, add half the beef. Fry for about 10 minutes, until browned all over, then remove with a slotted spoon and set aside. Repeat with the remaining beef.

3 Pour off most of the excess oil from the wok, leaving about 2 tablespoons. Add the lemon grass, spring onions, onion, ginger, garlic and dried chilli and stir-fry for 5 minutes. Transfer this mixture to a large casserole or saucepan. Add the browned beef and all the ingredients for the braising sauce.

4 Bring to the boil, skim off any fat from the surface, then turn the heat to a low simmer. Cover and braise for 1½–2 hours.

5 Add the carrots and continue to cook for 30 minutes, until the beef and carrots are tender. Remove the beef and carrots with a slotted spoon and set aside. Turn the heat up high and boil the liquid rapidly for about 15 minutes, until reduced and slightly thickened. Garnish with the chopped basil and mint and serve immediately. The stew can also be left to cool and then reheated later, garnished and served.

Indonesian dried beef curry

Known as *rendang*, this is probably one of Indonesia's most famous dishes. It appears on restaurant menus, as well as in many homes, and is unlike any other curry I have experienced. The meat is cooked in a highly aromatic sauce until the curry is dry. This rich and hearty dish reheats extremely well (with just a little water added) and can be made days in advance. In fact it is at its best a few days after it is made, as the meat gradually absorbs the flavours of the spices. It is perfect for entertaining a large crowd. Serve with plain rice and a vegetable or salad.

serves 4–6
preparation time: 40 minutes
cooking time: 3–3¹/₂ hours

2 onions, sliced

1 tablespoon coarsely chopped fresh ginger

6 garlic cloves, lightly crushed

1.2 litres (2 pints) canned coconut milk

1 kg (2¹/₄ lb) stewing beef (or lamb), such as brisket or shin, cut into 5 cm (2 in) cubes

2 tablespoons groundnut oil

2–3 teaspoons crushed dried red chilli

5 cloves

1 cinnamon stick

2 teaspoons salt

1 teaspoon freshly ground black pepper

1 tablespoon ground coriander

1 teaspoon ground cumin

1 teaspoon ground ginger

4 tablespoons lemon juice

1 Put half the onion in a blender with the ginger, garlic and 3–4 tablespoons of the coconut milk and blend until smooth. Put the meat in a large bowl, pour over the mixture from the blender and mix until the meat is thoroughly coated.

2 Heat a wok or large frying-pan, add the oil and, when it is very hot and slightly smoking, add the remaining onion. Stir-fry until golden brown. Using a slotted spoon, transfer the onion to a large casserole or saucepan.

3 Add half the meat to the wok and fry for about 10 minutes, until browned all over. Using a slotted spoon, transfer to the pan with the onions. Repeat with the remaining beef.

4 Add all the remaining ingredients except the lemon juice to the pan. Bring to a simmer and turn the heat as low as possible. Slowly braise, uncovered, for 2½–3 hours, stirring occasionally, until the beef is tender.

5 Stir in the lemon juice. The sauce should be quite thick now – almost dry. You can serve the curry immediately or you can leave it to cool and reheat it later.

Malaysian-style beef satay

Malaysian satay is spicier than the satays of Singapore. The flavours of India are apparent and, in a mainly Muslim culture, beef is used instead of pork. I like using beef fillet, as it is so tender. These satays are easy to prepare and make a lovely starter or an unusual accompaniment to drinks. For a main course, serve with rice and salad. The peanut sauce can be made way in advance and even freezes well.

serves 4
preparation time: 40 minutes, plus 1 hour's marinating
cooking time: 15–20 minutes

450 g (1 lb) beef fillet, cut into 2.5 cm (1 in) cubes

For the marinade:
3 tablespoons finely chopped shallots
2 tablespoons finely chopped garlic
1 tablespoon light soy sauce
1 tablespoon vegetable oil
1 teaspoon freshly ground black pepper
2 teaspoons ground turmeric
2 teaspoons ground cumin
2 teaspoons ground fennel seeds
1 teaspoon ground coriander
2 teaspoons sugar
2 teaspoons finely grated lemon zest
Salt

For the peanut sauce:
1 tablespoon groundnut oil
2 tablespoons coarsely chopped garlic
3 tablespoons coarsely chopped shallots
2 red chillies, seeded and chopped

1 tablespoon finely chopped fresh ginger
1 tablespoon lime or lemon juice
2 tablespoons coconut milk
1 tablespoon light soy sauce
1 teaspoon dark soy sauce
1 teaspoon sugar
250 ml (8 fl oz) water

175 g (6 oz) roasted peanuts, coarsely ground in a food processor
Salt and freshly ground black pepper

1 In a large bowl, combine the beef with all the marinade ingredients. Leave to marinate for 1 hour at room temperature.

2 Meanwhile, make the peanut sauce. Heat a wok or frying-pan, add the groundnut oil and, when it is slightly smoking, add the garlic, shallots, chillies and ginger and stir-fry for 1 minute. Then add the lime or lemon juice, coconut milk, light and dark soy sauce, sugar, water and some salt and pepper. Cook for 5 minutes, then add the coarsely ground peanuts and mix well.

3 Continue to simmer the sauce until you get the consistency you like. Add more water if you prefer it slightly thinner. Remove from the heat and leave to cool (the sauce should be served at room temperature).

4 Soak some bamboo skewers in cold water for 15 minutes. Thread the beef on to the skewers and set aside.

5 Prepare a barbecue or preheat a ridged chargrill pan or the oven grill. When the charcoal is ash white or the grill is very hot, cook the satay for 2 minutes on each side, or until done to your liking. Serve at once with the peanut sauce.

Singapore pork satay

Singapore is truly an East-meets-West 'fusion' city, with several different races and cultures merging harmoniously in that thriving modern metropolis. I love eating in Singapore and always make a point of visiting the street food stalls that sell so many different styles of food – from Chinese regional cuisine and indigenous Malay foods to authentic Indian treats.

A personal favourite is pork satay: tasty bits of meat marinated, skewered and simply grilled. This dish makes a wonderful main course or starter and you can easily double the recipe for a larger crowd.

serves 4
preparation time: 15 minutes,
  plus marinating overnight
cooking time: 15–20 minutes

450 g (1 lb) tender, thick
  boneless pork chops
1 quantity of Peanut Sauce
  (see pages 80–1)

For the marinade:
2 tablespoons light soy sauce
1 tablespoon Shaoxing rice
  wine or dry sherry

2 tablespoons finely chopped
  garlic
1 teaspoon freshly ground
  black pepper
2 teaspoons sesame oil
1 teaspoon sugar
2 teaspoons five-spice powder
Salt

3 The next day, soak some bamboo skewers in cold water for 15 minutes. Thread the pork on to the skewers and set aside.

1 Cut the pork into thin slices, about 2.5 cm (1 in) wide and 7.5 cm (3 in) long.

2 In a large bowl, combine the pork slices with all the marinade ingredients. Leave to marinate overnight in the fridge.

4 Prepare a barbecue or pre-heat a ridged grill pan or the oven grill. When the charcoal is ash white or the grill is very hot, cook the satay for 2 minutes on each side, until golden brown. Serve at once with the peanut sauce.

Vietnamese braised pork

This hearty, savoury dish has some affinities with a Chinese dish from Shanghai but is simpler to make. Vietnamese cooks use fish sauce instead of soy sauce, with a different but equally tasty result. An added bonus is that it reheats extremely well.

serves 6
preparation time: 15 minutes
cooking time: 1½ hours

About 3 tablespoons ground-nut oil

1 kg (2¼ lb) pork belly, including the rind, cut into 5 cm (2 in) pieces

6 spring onions, cut into 7.5 cm x 5 mm (3 x ¼ in) pieces

600 ml (1 pint) home-made chicken stock or good-quality bought stock

3 tablespoons sugar

1 teaspoon salt

2 teaspoons freshly ground black pepper

2 tablespoons fish sauce

1 Heat a wok or large frying-pan over a high heat. Add the oil and, when it is very hot and slightly smoking, fry the pieces of pork belly in it until they are crisp and brown all over (cover the wok to prevent splattering). Add more oil if necessary. Remove the pork from the wok and drain well.

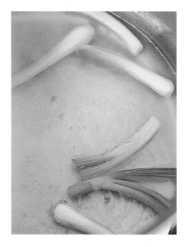

2 Put the spring onions, stock, sugar, salt and pepper into a large casserole and bring to a simmer.

3 Add the browned pork belly and simmer slowly, uncovered, for 1 hour, stirring occasionally. The mixture should become quite dry, but do watch that it doesn't burn. Stir in the fish sauce and cook for another 5 minutes, then serve.

Crispy Indonesian chicken

This Javanese-style fried chicken, known as *ayam goreng jawa*, is so popular in Indonesia that some restaurants serve nothing else. I remember the first time I ate it, outside Jakarta, and how delicious it was. The chicken is cooked in a savoury liquid, then deep-fried until crisp. Nothing could be tastier. The cooking can be done in advance and the deep-frying at the last moment when you are ready to serve the chicken. Plain rice and a salad make splendid accompaniments to this fine dish.

serves 4
preparation time: 25 minutes,
  plus cooling
cooking time: 30 minutes

400 ml (14 fl oz) canned
  coconut milk
900 g (2 lb) chicken thighs,
  with bone in
600 ml (1 pint) groundnut
  or vegetable oil, for
  deep-frying

For the paste:
1 fresh lemon grass stalk
1 teaspoon finely chopped
  fresh ginger
1 teaspoon freshly ground
  black pepper
2 tablespoons crushed garlic
3 fresh red chillies, seeded

3 Brazil nuts, shelled
2 teaspoons ground coriander
1 teaspoon salt
3 shallots, peeled
1/2 teaspoon ground turmeric
1 teaspoon sugar

1 First make the paste. Peel off the tough outer layers of the lemon grass stalk, leaving the tender, whitish centre. Crush with the flat of a knife, then chop finely.

2 Place the lemon grass stalk in a food processor with all the other ingredients for the paste, add half the coconut milk and blend until smooth. Pour this mixture into a large saucepan, together with the remaining coconut milk.

3 Blot the chicken thighs dry with kitchen paper and add to the pan. Bring to a simmer, turn the heat as low as possible, then cover and braise for 20 minutes.

4 Remove the chicken from the pan and leave to cool completely. The chicken can be cooked in advance to this point.

5 When you are ready to serve the chicken, heat a wok or deep saucepan over a high heat. Add the groundnut oil and, when it is very hot and slightly smoking, deep-fry the chicken, a few pieces at a time, until it is crisp and golden. Drain on kitchen paper, then serve at once.

Indonesian-style grilled spicy chicken

I remember the first time I saw this aromatic chicken dish being cooked on the streets of Jakarta. There, a small whole chicken is marinated and then slowly grilled. The smoky flavours, combined with the spices, were intoxicating. I find using chicken thighs works just as well. It makes a wonderful summer treat and can be served hot or at room temperature.

serves 4
preparation time: 45 minutes,
  plus marinating overnight
cooking time: 20 minutes

900 g (2 lb) chicken thighs,
  with bone in

For the marinade:

6 tablespoons finely chopped
  shallots

3 tablespoons coarsely
  chopped garlic

3 tablespoons finely grated
  lime or lemon zest

3 fresh red or green chillies,
  seeded and chopped

4 kaffir lime leaves, crushed,
  or 1 tablespoon finely
  grated lime zest

2 teaspoons finely chopped
  fresh ginger

1 teaspoon ground turmeric

2 teaspoons ground coriander

1 teaspoon salt

1 teaspoon freshly ground
  black pepper

5 tablespoons canned
  coconut milk

1 Combine all the marinade ingredients in a blender, food processor or a mortar and pestle and mix to a purée.

2 Blot the chicken thighs dry with kitchen paper, then put them in a large bowl. Add the marinade and mix well. Cover with cling film and leave to marinate in the fridge overnight.

3 Before you cook the chicken, remove it from the fridge and leave at room temperature for 40 minutes. Prepare a barbecue or preheat a ridged chargrill pan or the oven grill. When the charcoal is ash white or the grill is very hot, grill the chicken pieces for 10 minutes on each side or until they are cooked through. Place on a warm platter and serve immediately, or, if you prefer, allow to cool and serve at room temperature.

Ok, but not great

Stir-fried Indonesian-style chicken with vegetables

This is a typically hearty, family-style stir-fry dish that I have encountered numerous times in Jakarta. Indonesian cooks do not marinate their meat in the Chinese manner, with soy sauce, rice wine, etc. However, they often stir-fry it with pungent, aromatic ingredients such as shrimp paste and chillies. The results are just as tasty, and perfect for a large crowd.

serves 4–6
preparation time: 35 minutes
cooking time: 20 minutes

225 g (8 oz) broccoli

225 g (8 oz) asparagus

225 g (8 oz) button mushrooms

225 g (8 oz) baby sweetcorn

3 tablespoons groundnut or vegetable oil

450 g (1 lb) boneless, skinless chicken thighs, cut into 2.5 cm (1 in) pieces

2 tablespoons finely sliced garlic

3 tablespoons finely sliced shallots

2 large, fresh red chillies, seeded and sliced

1 tablespoon finely sliced fresh ginger

1½ tablespoons light soy sauce

2 teaspoons shrimp paste

2 teaspoons sugar

1 teaspoon salt

25 ml (1 fl oz) home-made chicken stock or good-quality bought stock, or water

Freshly ground black pepper

1 Cut the stalks off the broccoli and divide the heads into small florets. Peel and thinly slice the stalks on the diagonal.

2 Trim the woody ends off the asparagus and then cut into 4 cm (1½ in) lengths. Thinly slice the button mushrooms.

3 Blanch the broccoli and baby sweetcorn in a large pan of boiling salted water for 3 minutes. Drain and plunge them into cold water to stop them cooking further, then drain again.

4 Heat a wok or large frying-pan over a high heat. Add the oil and, when it is very hot and slightly smoking, add the chicken pieces and stir-fry for 5 minutes or until golden brown. Remove the chicken with a slotted spoon and leave to drain in a colander.

5 Reheat the wok over a high heat until it is medium hot. Add the garlic, shallots, chillies and ginger and stir-fry for about 2 minutes, until golden brown. Then add the soy sauce, shrimp paste, sugar, salt and pepper and stir-fry for 1 minute.

6 Now add the broccoli, corn, asparagus and mushrooms and continue to stir-fry for 3 minutes.

7 Return the drained chicken to the wok, add the stock or water and cook over a high heat for 5 minutes or until the chicken is thoroughly cooked. Turn out onto a platter and serve at once.

very good

Classic Vietnamese lemon grass chicken

In this hearty dish, lemon grass lends a fragrant flavour to chicken. It is quite easy to make and will satisfy a large, hungry family. Serve with noodles or rice.

serves 4–6
preparation time: 35 minutes,
 plus 45 minutes' marinating
cooking time: 20 minutes

1 small chicken, weighing about 900 g–1 kg (2–2¼ lb), jointed into small pieces (you could ask your butcher to do this)

5 fresh lemon grass stalks

1 teaspoon salt

½ teaspoon freshly ground black pepper

3 tablespoons finely chopped spring onions

2 tablespoons groundnut oil

175 g (6 oz) onions, finely sliced

6 garlic cloves, crushed

2 fresh red or green chillies, seeded and coarsely chopped

2 teaspoons sugar

100 g (4 oz) roasted peanuts, coarsely chopped

3 tablespoons fish sauce or light soy sauce

1 Blot the chicken dry with kitchen paper. Peel off the tough outer layers of the lemon grass stalks, leaving the tender, whitish centre. Crush with the flat of a knife, then cut into 7.5 cm (3 in) pieces.

2 In a large bowl, combine the chicken with the lemon grass, salt, pepper and spring onions. Leave to marinate at room temperature for 45 minutes.

3 Heat a wok or large frying-pan over a high heat. Add the oil and, when it is very hot and slightly smoking, add the chicken, together with the marinade ingredients, and stir-fry for 5 minutes. Then add the onions, garlic and chillies and continue to stir-fry for 10 minutes.

4 Add the sugar and peanuts and stir-fry for 2 minutes. Finally, add the fish sauce or light soy sauce and stir-fry for 2 minutes, mixing all the ingredients well. Transfer the mixture to a platter and serve at once.

Braised Balinese duck

I remember this dish, with its wonderful aroma, from my first visit to Bali in the early 1980s. It makes an ideal main course for a special occasion, and once the spice paste has been made, much of the work is done. Traditionally, the duck is stuffed with cassava leaves. These can be difficult, if not impossible, to find outside Bali, so I have left them out, without compromising the authentic flavour. The lovely savoury spices make a delicious contrast to the rich duck meat, producing a truly memorable feast. Serve with plain rice.

serves 4–6
preparation time: 45 minutes
cooking time: 3 hours

1 x 2.75 kg (6 lb) duck, fresh
   or frozen

For the spice paste:
2 fresh lemon grass stalks
4 garlic cloves, peeled
6 shallots, peeled
3 tablespoons coarsely
   chopped fresh galangal or
   ginger
6 red chillies, seeded
3 tablespoons lime juice
2 teaspoons coriander seeds
2 teaspoons cumin seeds
2 cloves
1 teaspoon ground cinnamon
1/2 teaspoon grated nutmeg
1/2 teaspoon ground turmeric
2 teaspoons shrimp paste
1/2 teaspoon freshly ground
   black pepper
2 teaspoons salt
2 tablespoons sesame oil
3 tablespoons water

1 If the duck is frozen, thaw it thoroughly. Rinse well and blot it completely dry with kitchen paper. Pre-heat the oven to 160°C/325°F/Gas Mark 3. Peel off the tough outer layers of the lemon grass stalks, leaving the tender, whitish centre. Crush with the flat of a knife, then cut into 7.5 cm (3 in) pieces. Put the lemon grass in a blender or food processor with all the remaining spice paste ingredients and blend as smoothly as possible.

2 Transfer the spice paste to a saucepan and simmer over a low heat for about 5 minutes, until thoroughly cooked, adding more water if the paste begins to stick to the pan.

3 Now rub the paste over the duck, inside and out. Carefully wrap the duck in several layers of foil, sealing it well.

4 Place the wrapped duck on a rack set over a roasting tin, pour a little water into the tin to prevent the fat splattering, and cook for 1 hour. Then turn the heat down to 140°C/275°F/Gas Mark 1 and continue to cook for 2 hours.

5 Remove the duck from the oven, unwrap it and pour any liquid into a heatproof glass bowl. Allow it to stand for a few minutes, then discard the surface fat, saving the juices.

6 Leave the duck to stand for at least 10 minutes before you carve it. Using a cleaver or a sharp knife, cut the skin and meat into pieces; it should be very tender. Arrange on a warm platter and serve at once, with the juices poured over the pieces.

VEGETABLES, SIDE DISHES and NOODLES

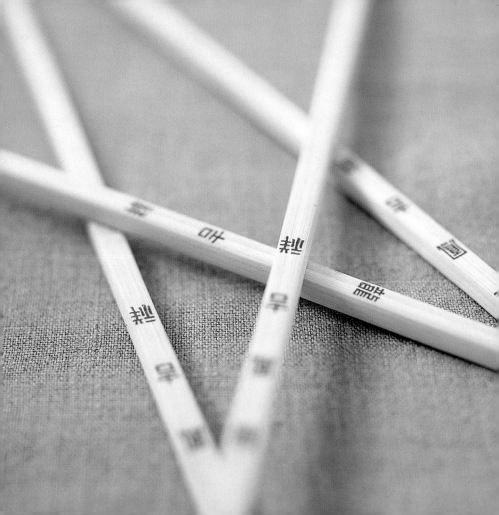

Vietnamese-style stir-fried vegetables

Every cuisine in the Far East has its own version of stir-fried vegetables. Here is the Vietnamese version, which shares some of the same vegetables as the Chinese one. Many varieties of lettuce are widely used in Vietnam, eaten fresh as salad, used to hold savoury foods such as spring rolls (see page 46), or even stir-fried, as in this recipe. I am sure it has been inspired by Vietnam's long Buddhist tradition.

When stir-frying vegetables, remember to begin with the firmer varieties that need more cooking time.

serves 4
preparation time: 25 minutes,
   plus 20 minutes' soaking
cooking time: 10 minutes

50 g (2 oz) Chinese dried mushrooms

225 g (8 oz) Chinese leaves (Peking cabbage)

225 g (8 oz) Cos lettuce

1 tablespoon vegetable oil

2 tablespoons coarsely chopped garlic

2 teaspoons finely chopped fresh ginger

3 tablespoons finely chopped spring onions

1 tablespoon dark soy sauce

1 1/2 tablespoons light soy sauce

2 teaspoons sugar

1 teaspoon salt

5 tablespoons water

1 Soak the dried mushrooms in warm water for 20 minutes, then drain them and squeeze out the excess liquid. Remove and discard the stalks and shred the caps into thin strips.

2 Cut the Chinese leaves and Cos lettuce into 4 cm (1 1/2 in) strips.

3 Heat a wok or large frying-pan over a high heat until it is medium hot. Add the oil, garlic and ginger and stir-fry for 1–1½ minutes, until golden brown. Now add the spring onions, dark and light soy sauce, sugar, salt and water, together with the mushrooms. Cook over a high heat for 2 minutes.

4 Add the Chinese leaves and stir-fry for 5 minutes, adding a little more water if necessary. Finally, stir in the lettuce and cook for another minute. Turn the vegetables on to a platter and serve at once.

Indonesian beancurd with peanuts

Although beancurd probably originated in China, it was brought to Indonesia by Chinese immigrants and embraced by local cooks. Here it is paired with peanuts, a very Indonesian food.

serves 4
preparation time: 30 minutes
cooking time: 20 minutes

450 g (1 lb) firm beancurd
450 ml (15 fl oz) groundnut oil for deep-frying, plus 1¹/₂ tablespoons
3 tablespoons peanut butter
2 tablespoons coarsely chopped garlic

2 small, fresh red chillies, seeded and chopped
1 teaspoon shrimp paste
2 tablespoons dark soy sauce
3 tablespoons lemon juice
1 teaspoon sugar
250 ml (8 fl oz) canned coconut milk

To garnish:
100 g (4 oz) fresh bean sprouts, rinsed
50 g (2 oz) roasted peanuts, coarsely chopped
1 spring onion, shredded

1 Cut the beancurd into 2.5 cm (1 in) cubes and drain on kitchen paper.

2 Heat the 450 ml (15 fl oz) oil in a large wok until it is almost smoking, then deep-fry the beancurd cubes in it in 2 batches. When each batch is lightly browned, remove and drain well on kitchen paper. Let the cooking oil cool and then discard it.

3 Wipe the wok clean and reheat it over a high heat. Add the 1¹/₂ tablespoons of oil and, when it is very hot and smoking, add the peanut butter, garlic, chillies and shrimp paste and stir-fry for 1 minute.

4 Add the drained beancurd. Stir-fry for 30 seconds, then add the dark soy sauce, lemon juice, sugar and coconut milk. Reduce the heat to low and simmer the mixture slowly for 8 minutes.

5 Raise the heat again and cook until most of the liquid has evaporated. Place the beancurd on a serving platter, cover with the bean sprouts, then sprinkle on the peanuts and spring onion and serve at once.

Malaysian vegetable curry

Although one can detect an Indian influence in this typical Malaysian dish, the flavours are unique. What makes a great difference is the use of shrimp paste, an aromatic seasoning found in many Malaysian vegetable dishes. When it is combined with chillies, the results are sensational. There is a secret, however, to this recipe: do not add all the vegetables at the same time. Like stir-frying, stewing requires you to give different vegetables different cooking times. If the cooking times are properly observed, the whole dish comes out perfectly done.

serves 4
preparation time: 20 minutes
cooking time: 20 minutes

2 x 400 ml (14 fl oz) cans of coconut milk

100 g (4 oz) onion, finely sliced

1 tablespoon finely chopped garlic

1/2 teaspoon shrimp paste

1/2 teaspoon ground turmeric

2 fresh red or green chillies, seeded and sliced

1 teaspoon salt

1/2 teaspoon freshly ground black pepper

175 g (6 oz) potatoes, peeled and sliced

350 g (12 oz) Chinese leaves (Peking cabbage), shredded

1 tablespoon lemon juice

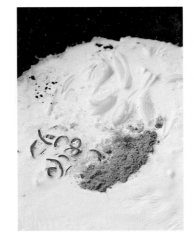

1 Pour the coconut milk into a wok or large frying-pan and bring to a simmer. Add the onion, garlic, shrimp paste, turmeric, chillies, salt and pepper and return to a simmer.

2 Add the potatoes and cook for 8 minutes, until they are almost tender, then add the Chinese leaves. Cover and simmer for 6 minutes, until they are thoroughly cooked.

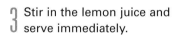

3 Stir in the lemon juice and
serve immediately.

Stir-fried Singapore water spinach

My good friend Jenny Lo, who is Malaysian–Chinese, introduced me to this delicious, earthy dish. I have since eaten it numerous times in Singapore. Water spinach is a leafy vegetable that is prolific throughout Southeast Asia. It is similar to ordinary spinach, which can easily be substituted. However, the appeal of water spinach is the crunchy, hollow stalk, which is just as tasty as the leaves. You can find water spinach in Chinese supermarkets.

> serves 2–4
> preparation time: 20 minutes
> cooking time: 10 minutes

675 g (1¹/₂ lb) water spinach
  or ordinary spinach
2 tablespoons groundnut or
  vegetable oil
2 teaspoons shrimp paste
50 g (2 oz) shallots, finely
  sliced

5 garlic cloves, finely sliced
2 fresh red chillies, seeded
  and chopped
1 teaspoon sugar
Salt and freshly ground black
  pepper

1 If you are using water spinach, wash it thoroughly. Trim any tough ends off the stalks. If you are using ordinary spinach, wash it thoroughly and remove and discard the stalks.

2 Heat a wok or large frying-pan over a high heat, add the oil and, when it is very hot and slightly smoking, add the shrimp paste and crush it in the hot oil.

3 Add the shallots and garlic and stir-fry for 2–3 minutes, until they are lightly browned.

4 Add the chillies, sugar and spinach. Stir-fry for about 2 minutes to coat the spinach thoroughly with the aromatic mixture.

5 After the spinach has wilted to about one-third of its original size, continue to stir-fry for 4 minutes. Season with salt and pepper, transfer the spinach to a plate and pour off any excess liquid. Serve immediately.

Indonesian-style green bean sambal

This is one of the tastiest recipes I know for green beans. Indonesian spicing gives it a real kick. *Sambal* simply means 'spice mixture', and there are many different types.

serves 2–4
preparation time: 20 minutes
cooking time: 10 minutes

2 small, fresh red chillies, seeded and chopped

1 tablespoon cider vinegar

1½ tablespoons groundnut oil

450 g (1 lb) runner beans or French beans, trimmed and cut into 7.5 cm (3 in) lengths

2 teaspoons coarsely chopped garlic

3 tablespoons water

1 small red onion, finely sliced

Salt

1 Place the chillies, vinegar, 1 tablespoon of water and some salt in a food processor or blender and purée to a smooth paste, adding more water if necessary. Set aside.

2 Heat a wok or large frying-pan over a high heat until it is hot. Add the oil and, when it is very hot and slightly smoking, add the beans and stir-fry for 30 seconds.

3 Add the puréed chilli mixture, plus the garlic, water and some salt. Stir-fry for 1 minute.

4 Cover the wok and cook for 5 minutes or until the beans are tender. Uncover and stir-fry until all the liquid has evaporated. Mix in the sliced red onion and serve at once.

Indonesian-style sweetcorn fritters

Here is an engaging starter – an enticing blend of sweetcorn and seasonings, all fried into crispy morsels. They make a lovely first course for any meal. If you are preparing the fritters for a dinner party, you could partially fry them beforehand and then plunge them into hot oil again just before serving.

serves 4–6
preparation time: 40 minutes
cooking time: about 15 minutes

450 g (1 lb) corn on the cob,
    or 275 g (10 oz) can of plain
    sweetcorn

5 shallots, finely sliced

2 tablespoons finely chopped
    spring onions

2 tablespoons finely chopped
    garlic

1 teaspoon ground coriander

1/2 teaspoon ground cumin

2 teaspoons salt

1/2 teaspoon freshly ground
    white pepper

1 teaspoon sugar

4 tablespoons rice flour or
    plain flour

1 teaspoon baking powder

2 eggs, beaten

600 ml (1 pint) groundnut oil,
    for deep-frying

2 tablespoons finely chopped
    fresh coriander, or a few
    whole leaves

1 If using corn on the cob, remove the husks and slice off the kernels with a sharp knife or cleaver. You should end up with about 275 g (10 oz) corn kernels. If you are using canned corn, drain it thoroughly.

2 In a blender or food processor, combine half the corn with all the rest of the ingredients except the groundnut oil and fresh coriander. Blend to a purée, pour this mixture into a bowl and mix in the rest of the corn. Leave the mixture to stand for at least 5 minutes.

3 Heat a wok or deep saucepan over a high heat. Add the oil and, when it is very hot and slightly smoking, ladle a large spoon-sized portion of the sweetcorn mixture into it. Repeat until the wok is full.

4 Reduce the heat to medium and cook the fritters for about 2 minutes, until golden brown underneath. Turn them over and fry the other side, then remove with a slotted spoon and drain on kitchen paper. Repeat with the remaining sweetcorn mixture. Arrange the fritters on a warm platter, garnish with the chopped coriander (or whole leaves) and serve at once.

Indonesian fried rice

This is the famous Indonesian *nasi goreng* – a truly delectable one-meal rice dish that is made simply in a wok. Unlike the Chinese version of fried rice, it includes a combination of meat and prawns. There is also the addition of soy sauce and shrimp paste, which is uniquely Indonesian. It is typical of the rich and flavourful food one finds in Indonesia.

serves 4–6
preparation time: 30 minutes
cooking time: 30 minutes

Long-grain white rice, measured to the 400 ml (14 fl oz) level in a measuring jug

2 eggs, beaten

2 teaspoons sesame oil

1 teaspoon salt

2 tablespoons groundnut oil

2 tablespoons coarsely chopped garlic

175 g (6 oz) raw prawns, shelled and de-veined (see pages 16–17), then cut into 1 cm (1/2 in) pieces

1 small onion, finely chopped

1 tablespoon shrimp paste

225 g (8 oz) minced pork or beef

1 tablespoon light soy sauce

2 teaspoons dark soy sauce

1 small cucumber, peeled and finely sliced

Freshly ground black pepper

1 At least 2 hours in advance, or even the night before, cook the rice according to the instructions on page 17. Allow it to cool thoroughly and then put it in the refrigerator.

2 Combine the eggs with the sesame oil, half the salt and some black pepper, then set aside.

3 Heat a wok or large frying-pan over a high heat. Add the oil and, when it is very hot and slightly smoking, add the garlic, prawns, onion, shrimp paste, the remaining salt and some black pepper. Stir-fry for 2 minutes.

4 Add the minced pork or beef and stir-fry for 2 minutes. Now add the rice and continue to stir-fry for 3 minutes. Next, add the light soy sauce and dark soy sauce and stir-fry for 2 minutes.

5 Add the egg mixture and stir-fry for another minute. Turn on to a platter, garnish with the sliced cucumber and serve.

Malaysian curry *mee*

Malaysia is a culinary crossroads of cuisines, spices and ingredients, with Chinese and Indian flavours in particular merging into a distinctly national style of cooking. A popular Malaysian recipe is this simple but delectable egg noodle dish (the word *mee* refers to the noodles). It combines bean sprouts and beancurd – standard ingredients used by Chinese cooks – with a light curry sauce that manifests the Indian influence. It makes a delicious one-dish meal all by itself.

serves 4
preparation time: 20 minutes, plus 30 minutes' draining
cooking time: 20 minutes

450 g (1 lb) firm beancurd

225 g (8 oz) dried or fresh Chinese egg noodles

1 tablespoon vegetable oil

2 tablespoons groundnut oil

2 dried red chillies, halved

2 tablespoons coarsely chopped garlic

100 g (4 oz) onion, finely chopped

400 ml (14 fl oz) canned coconut milk

1/2 teaspoon ground turmeric

2 tablespoons Madras curry powder

1 teaspoon salt

1 teaspoon sugar

2 tablespoons light soy sauce

1 tablespoon dark soy sauce

225 g (8 oz) fresh bean sprouts, rinsed

Freshly ground black pepper

1 Cut the beancurd into 2.5 cm (1 in) cubes, then leave on kitchen paper to drain for 30 minutes.

2 Cook the noodles for 3–5 minutes in a pan of boiling water, until tender. Drain and plunge them into cold water. Drain again thoroughly and toss them with the vegetable oil, then set aside.

3 Heat a wok or large frying-pan over a high heat. Add the groundnut oil and, when it is very hot and slightly smoking, add the dried chillies and stir-fry for 20 seconds. Push the chillies to the side of the wok, lower the heat and add the beancurd cubes. Brown slowly on each side.

4 Add the garlic and onion and stir-fry for 3 minutes, until the onion is soft. Now add the coconut milk, turmeric, curry powder, salt, sugar, light and dark soy sauce and some black pepper and simmer for 4 minutes.

5 Finally, add the noodles and bean sprouts, cook for 2 minutes and mix well. Serve at once.

Singapore classic *laksa*

The word *laksa* in Malaysian describes a one-dish meal of rice noodles, traditionally prepared with either seafood or chicken. I first tasted it over 20 years ago, on my first trip to Singapore. I was a poor student and it filled my stomach and satisfied my craving for a hearty, tasty, aromatic noodle dish. It is a fantastic dish to make for a large crowd.

serves 4–6
preparation time: 40 minutes
cooking time: 35 minutes

2 fresh lemon grass stalks

1½ tablespoons oil, preferably groundnut oil

2 tablespoons coarsely chopped garlic

1 tablespoon finely chopped fresh ginger

2–3 small, fresh red chillies, seeded and finely shredded

225 g (8 oz) shallots, finely sliced

1 teaspoon ground coriander

½ teaspoon ground turmeric

1 teaspoon salt

1.2 litres (2 pints) home-made chicken stock or good-quality bought stock

225 g (8 oz) rice noodles, rice vermicelli or rice sticks

400 ml (14 fl oz) canned coconut milk

2 teaspoons Madras curry powder

2 teaspoons shrimp paste

1 teaspoon sugar

½ teaspoon freshly ground black pepper

450 g (1 lb) raw prawns, shelled and de-veined (see pages 16–17)

To garnish:

3 tablespoons finely sliced spring onions

200 g (7 oz) bean sprouts, blanched in boiling water for 30 seconds, then drained

4 quail's eggs, hard-boiled, shelled and cut in half (or use 2 hen's eggs)

1 lime or lemon, cut into wedges

Sprigs of fresh coriander and mint

1 Peel off the tough outer layers of the lemon grass stalks, leaving the tender, whitish centre. Crush with the flat of a knife, then cut into 7.5 cm (3 in) pieces.

2 Heat a wok or large frying-pan over a high heat, add the oil and, when it is very hot and slightly smoking, add the lemon grass, garlic, ginger, chillies and shallots and stir-fry for 5 minutes.

3 Now add the ground coriander, turmeric, salt and stock. Reduce the heat to low, cover and simmer for 20 minutes.

4 Meanwhile, soak the rice noodles in a bowl of warm water for 20 minutes. Drain them in a colander or sieve.

5 Add the coconut milk and rice noodles to the simmering stock. Season with the curry powder, shrimp paste, sugar, and black pepper, add the prawns and continue to simmer for 10 minutes. Ladle the mixture into a large soup tureen and serve at once, with the garnishes on the side.

Northern Vietnamese aromatic beef noodle soup

This popular dish is said to have originated in Hanoi and is commonly known as *pho*, meaning 'in one's bowl'. There are as many versions of *pho* in Vietnam as there are cooks. However, this is as close to the original as they come. Rich and satisfying in flavour, it makes a hearty accompaniment or one-dish meal. The secret lies in the strong beef stock that results from long simmering. It is eaten at all times of the day or night and the aromatic garnishes are part of its charm.

> serves 4
> preparation time: 30 minutes
> cooking time: 3¹/₂ hours

1 kg (2¹/₄ lb) beef brisket or shin (with some fat and tendon), cut into 4 cm (1¹/₂ in) cubes

3 slices of fresh ginger

2 onions, sliced

1 cinnamon stick

1 teaspoon black peppercorns

3 star anise

1.75 litres (3 pints) home-made chicken or beef stock or good-quality bought stock

225 g (8 oz) thin or flat dried rice noodles

225 g (8 oz) tender beef fillet, cut into very thin slices

Salt

To garnish:

225 g (8 oz) bean sprouts, blanched in boiling water for 30 seconds, then drained

4 fresh red or green chillies, seeded and chopped

2 limes or lemons, cut into wedges

4 spring onions, chopped

Sprigs of fresh coriander

Fresh basil leaves

Fish sauce

Freshly ground black pepper

1 Bring a large pot of salted water to the boil. Add the pieces of beef brisket or shin and simmer gently for 10 minutes, constantly skimming the scum and impurities from the surface. Drain the meat and discard the water.

2 Put the blanched beef back in the pot, then add the ginger, onions, cinnamon, peppercorns, star anise and stock. Bring the mixture to a simmer, then reduce the heat to low, cover and cook slowly for 3 hours, until the meat is very tender. The soup can be prepared in advance to this point; indeed, even days before.

3 Soak the noodles in a large bowl of warm water for 15 minutes, until soft. Drain and discard the water.

4 When the meat is cooked, strain the broth into a clean pan, discarding the beef. Skim off any surface fat and season with salt to taste.

5 Add the noodles to the broth, return to the boil and simmer for 3 minutes. When you are ready to serve the *pho*, arrange the slices of beef fillet in a large tureen or large individual soup bowls. Ladle the hot broth and rice noodles into the tureen or bowls and leave to stand for 3 minutes, in order to cook the beef lightly. Then serve the soup with all the garnishes arranged on a platter. The idea is for each guest to add their choice of garnishes and seasoning to their soup.

Menus

Dining in Indonesia, Malaysia, Singapore and Vietnam is a rather informal affair. A meal can be as simple as a quick roadside snack of noodles, or a lengthier affair that involves sitting down with family members or friends. Unlike in Europe, dishes are usually served in the middle of the table, whether they be appetizers or main courses, together with vegetables and usually rice. These are often shared. A few suggested menus and themes follow that reflect the rich culinary heritage of Southeast Asia.

Southeast Asian Vegetarian

Vietnamese-style Stir-fried Vegetables

Indonesian-style Sweetcorn Fritters

Malaysian Curry *Mee*

Home Cooking

Singapore-style Oyster Omelette

Indonesian Dried Beef Curry

Plain Steamed Rice

Street Foods

Grilled Indonesian Prawn Skewers

Singapore-style Chilli Crab

Malaysian-style Beef Satay

Summer Menu

Fresh Vietnamese Spring Rolls

Warm Vietnamese Beef Salad

Indonesian-style Grilled Spicy Chicken

Easy Entertaining

Vietnamese Beef and Spinach Soup

Malaysian Prawn Fritters

Stir-fried Singapore Water Spinach

Elegant Dinner Party

Crispy Vietnamese Spring Rolls

Malaysian Black Bean Fish

Indonesian Fried Rice

Healthy Southeast Asian

Vietnamese Soup with Beancurd

Indonesian Vegetable Salad

Singapore-style Steamed Fish

Hearty Menu

Indonesian-style Chicken Soup

Malaysian Fish Curry

Vietnamese-style Beef Stew

Index

Acknowledgements

An author of a book is just the front person. There are countless of people in the background that make every book possible. All are impossible to name; however, here are some of the most important ones. I am fortunate to be blessed with the greatest team at BBC Books, beginning with Viv Bowler, my commissioning editor and her able assistant Vicki Vrint; Sarah Lavelle, the project editor, who makes sure all the bits comes together; and of course,

Jane Middleton as copy editor who catches all the inconsistencies. The *Foolproof* series has been such a success because of Lisa Pettibone as designer; Jean Cazals' beautiful and accurate photography and Marie Ange Lapierre as the home economist, together with Sue Rowlands as the food stylist. None of my book projects would be successful without Gordon Wing's precise testing of all the recipes and my agent, Carole Blake, without whom I could not live.